Liberia Plantation, Manassas, March 1862.

MANASSAS MOSAIC:
Creating a Community

THE
DONNING COMPANY
PUBLISHERS

MANASSAS MOSAIC:
Creating a Community

By Rita G. Koman

Unless otherwise acknowledged, all images are from the Manassas Museum System's collections.

The Donning Company Publishers
184 Business Park Drive, Suite 206
Virginia Beach, VA 23462

Steve Mull, General Manager
Barbara Buchanan, Office Manager
Pamela Koch, Senior Editor
Chad Casey, Graphic Designer
Derek Eley, Imaging Artist
Lori Porter, Project Research Coordinator
Tonya Hannink, Marketing Specialist
Pamela Engelhard, Marketing Advisor

Dennis N. Walton, Project Director

Library of Congress Cataloging-in-Publication Data

Koman, Rita G.
Manassas mosaic : creating a community / by Rita G. Koman.
p. cm.
Includes bibliographical references and index.
ISBN 978-1-57864-583-1 (hard cover : alk. paper)
1. Manassas (Va.)—History. I. Title.
F234.M2K66 2009
975.5'2734—dc22
2009026238

Printed in the United States of America at Walsworth Publishing Company

Contents

Foreword

Crossroads of the Piedmont aptly describes the community that began its life with its roots deeply embedded in the rich red soil and mild climate of the region. Native Americans hunted and fished here for thousands of years before the European colonists came to clear the land for agriculture. It was not until the middle of the nineteenth century and the arrival of the railroad and the American Civil War that the town of Manassas began to emerge as a community.

Throughout the eighteenth and nineteenth centuries, large plantations and small farms populated the countryside around present-day Manassas, which began its written history as Tudor Hall, a village where two railroads joined in the 1850s. Later named Manassas Junction and then simply Manassas, the town developed shortly after the Civil War. Its railroad lines provided transportation for goods and people to Alexandria and Washington, D.C.

Today, the city of Manassas occupies ten square miles of Prince William County and has about thirty-five thousand residents. Although the surrounding community is often included when describing Manassas, we cannot recount the history of Manassas without recognizing that historical events often ignore such boundaries.

The City of Manassas theme is "Rich in Historical Interest." Turn-of-the-century buildings still grace the narrow main streets of Old Town. Frequent festivals enliven the community, while an old-fashioned Christmas parade each December and a spectacular and patriotic fireworks display on July Fourth bring crowds from throughout Northern Virginia and the Washington, D.C., metropolitan area.

This book will give the reader an opportunity to learn about the rich and fascinating history of Manassas gleaned from the resources of the Manassas Museum System archives, the Library of Virginia, and many other community resources.

John H. Verrill
Director of Historic Resources
Manassas Museum System

Acknowledgments

I can trace my interest in the history of Manassas back to my days as an American history teacher at Osbourn High School in the 1980s. I had my eleventh-grade students "dig up" historical information about the city, and although they uncovered some interesting facts, the first museum curator, Doug Harvey, imparted a sense of order to the information. The more I researched Manassas history, the more I realized I wanted to write a succinct, thorough history of Manassas. In July 2006, the opportunity presented itself when Manassas Museum System contracted with the Donning Company to publish this book. Using the museum's extensive resources made my research a fascinating journey through our past. The result is a local history from the earliest settlements into the present.

Although my efforts have been a labor of love for our local history, I could not have produced this book without the invaluable assistance of many people. First and foremost, I thank Roxana Adams, the curator of the Manassas Museum System who encouraged me to undertake the project and spent countless hours reviewing my efforts, helping select and sort photographs, adding to captions, editing text, and giving encouragement. Without her, the manuscript and photographs would never have been put in the mail.

Manassas Museum staff members John Verrill, director, and Vina Hutchinson read the first completed draft as did Don Wilson, Virginiana Librarian at the Prince William County's Bull Run Regional Library. Don and his colleagues Tish Como and Beverly Veness were of immense help in finding pre–Civil War information. Dr. Robert Wilson, editor of *The American Scholar*, reviewed several early chapters. Margaret and David Binning skillfully indexed the book.

I have had the continuing good fortune to know Ann Walser Harrover Thomas, who has family roots in Manassas prior to the Civil War days. Her personal knowledge of Manassas was invaluable. Papers accumulated by Roberta Plaster of the Hooe family gave further insight into the earliest days of Prince William County. Many Manassas property owners allowed their homes to be photographed so my words could be brought to life through pictures. The modern photographs of Larry Bates and Don Flory bring the book full circle to the present.

Over time, the hamlet Manassas grew to become the city of thousands in which we live today. To my ever-patient husband who thought this book would never see the "light of day," I thank you for your support and endurance over the "long haul." My hope is that readers will gain new insight into our city's past and receive pleasure from reading about its continuing development.

Rita G. Koman

Chapter I

The Northern Piedmont, Its Setting, and Its People

Prehistoric–1800

An early artist's depiction of the eastern coastline as ships arrived in the Chesapeake Bay heading for Virginia. (The Library of Virginia)

Centuries before the first Englishmen ventured onto the shores of North America, various Native American tribes roamed Virginia's Northern Piedmont, the land at the foot of the mountains, some as early as 7000 BC. The hills along Bull Run Mountains were hunting grounds for nomadic Manahoac Indians. Periodically,

Indian points found on the eastern Prince William County property of Jerry MacDonald. They were part of Native American hunting equipment about 8000–7000 BC.

these tribes burned the forested areas to promote grass growth for deer, elk, and buffalo. Toward the east and south, Dogue (Doeg, Doog, Toag, Taux) or Algonquin Indians lived along the Occoquan Bay and Mason Neck peninsula. The Necostins (Nactachtanks, Anacostins, or Alqonquins) made their home along the Potomac. As members of the Powhatan Confederacy, they were called Manahoacs/Piedmonts and Dogues and spoke a Siouan dialect. They were stable inhabitants. In land where western Prince William County and Manassas are today, hunters roamed near the waters of Flat Branch and Winters Branch, sources for springs. As they passed through the area, war parties of the Five Nations of the Iroquois often followed a path near Gainesville that came to be called Old Carolina Road by white men. Collectively, these tribes represented a mixture of northern and southern Native cultures.

Exploring the upper Tidewaters of Virginia in 1608, John Smith was the first Englishman to see a King's House of the Dogues as he sailed into Occoquan Bay. He arrived at the village of Pamacocock at the mouth of the Chappawamic Creek and visited a village called Tauxnent on the Occoquan roughly in the area of Dumfries and Occoquan. Smith described the area as rich in fish and wildlife, especially below the geographical fall line of the Potomac River. Advertising Virginia as a cornucopia of wildlife, fish, and geese, and lauding the Natives for planting abundant crops of corn, potatoes, pumpkins, and beans, Smith's descriptions went unchallenged in England.

As early as 1640, John Mottrom, probably the first Englishman to settle on the Virginia side of the Potomac River, settled on the York River of the Lower Northern Neck of Northumberland County. He would become the first man from Northern Virginia to

Above: Lady Catherine Culpeper (1670–1719) was the only surviving child of her father and inherited his extensive lands in Virginia. (Courtesy of Leeds Castle, Kent, England)

Far right: Lord Thomas Fairfax, the Fifth Lord (1657–1710), married Lady Catherine Culpeper and assumed ownership of her inherited land. (Courtesy of Jon Kukla)

represent the area in the Virginia House of Burgesses. Subsequent years saw four other counties, Lancaster (1651) , Westmoreland (1653), Rappahannock (1656), and Richmond (1692), develop between these two transportation waterways. In 1664, Stafford County was the furthest western county in the Northern Neck formed from Westmoreland County.

Years of negotiation with displaced Native Americans led to the 1722 Treaty of Albany under the Virginia governorship of Alexander Spotswood. In summary, the Five Nations of the Iroquois agreed to never appear on the land south of the Potomac and east of the Blue Ridge Mountains on threat of death or enslavement in the West Indies.

The land from which Prince William County would be carved was part of a six-million-acre grant that the exiled English King Charles II gave to seven Royalist supporters in 1649: Ralph Lord Hopton, John Lord Culpeper, Sir John Berkeley, Sir William Morton, Sir Dudley Wyatt, Thomas Culpeper, and Henry Lord Jermyn. The gift of land stretched from the Potomac River to the Rappahannock River and began in the east with the Chesapeake Bay. The western frontier lands had no specified borders. Terms of the grant stipulated that the new grantees give the Crown

one-tenth of all the silver and one-fifth of all the gold found plus an annual rental fee of six pounds, thirteen shillings, and four pence ($376.72 in 2009 U.S. dollars). This magnificent gift immediately opened up the Piedmont to thousands of settlers and speculators from the lower Virginia Tidewater.

By 1660, Charles II, out of exile now, was attempting to control runaway speculation by many of the colony's most elite. He made a second grant in 1673 that only confused the situation by giving overlapping claims to the Earl of Arlington and Lord Culpeper. In addition, some of the first grantees died without making their claims. Royal Governor Sir William Berkeley's attention was focused on keeping his governorship in the face of Bacon's Rebellion (1676), which was precipitated by Berkeley's failure to defend the frontier against attacks by Native Americans.

Robert "King" Carter (1663-1732). Carter was Lord Fairfax's agent. He administered and maintained the Fairfax Proprietary. From an original portrait at Sabine Hall. (Courtesy of Historic Christ Church.)

Ultimately, the proprietary grant was realigned and in the hands of Thomas Fairfax, second Lord Culpeper, Baron of Thoresway and Thomas, fifth Baron of Cameron. In 1689, Catherine Culpeper, his only heir, inherited the land. Within a year, she married Lord Fairfax, and under the law he became the owner of his wife's property. To maintain and administer the property, in 1702 Fairfax hired Robert "King" Carter of Lancaster County as his Virginia agent; Carter acted in this capacity until his death in 1732.

By now, a modification in colony law put authority over the Fairfax proprietary and the rest of the colony in the hands of the Royal Governor and the General Assembly. When Thomas Fairfax, sixth Lord Fairfax of Cameron inherited the proprietary upon his father's death, King George I ordered the land to be surveyed. While Carter continued to be his agent, Fairfax moved to Virginia in 1735 to inspect and protect his lands. Quitrents (taxes) went directly to Fairfax not to the colony.

Controversy over the extent of the Fairfax Proprietary led to a review by the British Board of Trade, which recommended a survey to resolve the southern and western boundaries of the

Prince William County was named for His Royal Highness Prince William Augustus, Duke of Cumberland and son of King George II. He is portrayed here at the age of ten, one year after the county was named for him. Photograph of a painting by Charles Jervas. (Courtesy of the National Portrait Gallery, London, England)

proprietary. Fairfax went to England in 1737 to argue his case before the King's Privy Council. He returned victorious in 1745. Based on the survey, the Privy Council determined Fairfax's claim to be 5.2 million acres. This award gave him quitrents from the entire Northern Neck plus land stretching across much of northern Virginia and into several counties now in West Virginia. The ruling was effective until the American Revolution.

Meanwhile, the area quickly filled up with settlers, leading to a request to increase the number of counties. In 1730, there was a new procedure in which, to create a new county, the Assembly would first create a new parish and then a new county whose boundaries were the same as those of the parish. In this manner, Hamilton Parish was created by Act of the General Assembly of Virginia on January 1, 1731, and became Prince William County, established on March 25, 1731.

According to the Act:

"All the lands on the head of the said counties, above Chopawansick [*sic*] Creek on Potomac River and Deep Run on Rappahannock River and southwest line to be made from the head of the north branch of the said creek, . . . be made a distinct county and shall be called and known by the name of Prince William County."

Most of the population was centered on the south side of Occoquan Creek near present-day Woodbridge. Thus, the county seat was placed there. By 1759, Dumfries became an important seaport and county seat. No northern or western limits were set allowing the assumption that ultimately the Blue Ridge Mountains and the north fork of the Rappahannock would serve as extreme boundaries.

Prince William County was named for William Augustus (1721–1765), King George II's second surviving son, who was nine years old at the time. William bore the title Duke of Cumberland, and upon coming of age in 1742, he was made a major general in the English army. Serving in the battle of Dettingen, Germany, where he was wounded, a large portion of Prince William County was named Dettingen Parish of the Church of England in his honor. The following counties would separate from Prince William over time: Fairfax (1742), Loudoun (1757), Fauquier (1759), and Arlington (1920).

His Royal Highness Prince William as an adult. As a leading British general, he successfully put a decisive stop to the successful career of Charles Edward Stuart, known as "the Young Pretender," in the Jacobite Rebellion of 1745. Many locations in America were also named "Cumberland" after His Highness.

The Indian threat in the county was effectively eliminated by 1724 allowing "King" Carter to patent approximately ninety thousand acres in present-day Prince William, Fairfax, Fauquier, and Loudoun counties in the name of his own sons, grandsons, and other relatives. The Lower Bull Run Tract of 6,730 acres went to his son George Carter, encompassing most of present-day Manassas, Manassas Park, Yorkshire, West Gate, and lands on both sides of Interstate 66. As a youth, George Washington surveyed these lands for Lord Fairfax.

As the seventeenth century progressed in Prince William County, George Washington escorted General Braddock overland through the area to his certain death at the hands of the Indians and French in western Pennsylvania in 1755. In 1774, shortly after the Boston Tea Party, residents at the Dumfries courthouse went on record opposing the Stamp Act by penning the *Prince William Resolves.* The *Resolves* opposed taxation without representation,

Virginia has a gold belt running from the Great Falls on the Potomac River, south and west into North Carolina, stretching through Prince William, Orange, Fairfax, Fauquier, Culpeper, and Goochland counties. This belt was one of the richest stores of gold in the country prior to the discovery of ore in California in the 1840s. The first gold discovery was at White Hall in 1806. Almost fifty gold mines opened and operated during the span of more than one hundred years: 1829–1940s.

foretelling the Declaration of Independence two years later. Continuous westward movement spread the population further into the county. Colonel Thomas Lee, eldest son of Senator Richard Henry Lee of the Continental Congress, built Park Gate in the vicinity of present-day Nokesville about 1790. Here, he and his wife, Mildred Washington, a niece of George Washington, lived until 1805.

As tensions grew between the colonies and Great Britain, prominent citizens formed a Committee of Safety in preparation for possible war. Once involved in conflict, Lee carried secret documents for General Washington to his uncle, Arthur Lee, an envoy in France. He also served as an aide-de-camp to Washington. Other revolutionary residents included William Grayson, Thomas Blackburn, Howson Hooe, Jesse Ewell, Cuthbert Harrison, William Brent, and John Peyton. William Grayson, for whom the local chapter of the Sons of the American Revolution is named, served as first captain of the Prince William Independent Company of Cadets, formed in 1774 by the young gentry of the county. Henry Lee and Thomas Blackburn represented the county at St. John's Church, witnessing Patrick Henry's famous "Give me liberty or give me death" speech. Grayson later also became an aide-de-camp to General Washington. Among the many recruits from Prince William County, James Nickens Sr., a free black, fought as a soldier in the army. Henry Dogan fought with the Eleventh Regiment of Foot and saw action at Valley Forge.

Upon successful conclusion of the Revolutionary War, Virginia operated under a new state constitution drawn up under the major supervision of George Mason of Fairfax. Each county got two delegates to sit in the General Assembly. Cuthbert Bullitt of Mount View Plantation and Jesse Ewell, Bel Air Plantation, were Prince William's first chosen delegates. When Virginians pushed to reexamine the Articles of Confederation, first at Mount Vernon, then in Annapolis, and later in Philadelphia, the county sent Grayson and Bullitt as representatives. Interestingly, while Virginia ultimately became the tenth state to adopt the federal constitution, Prince William delegates voted against it. Nevertheless, Virginia chose William Grayson to serve with Richard Henry Lee as the first two U.S. senators from the state. Grayson was responsible for inserting the clause prohibiting slavery into the Northwest Ordinance of 1787.

Westward population shifts led to the establishment of Buckland (1796) and Haymarket (1799) as towns. Dumfries, chartered in 1749, was the judicial district for Prince William, Fauquier, Fairfax, and Loudoun counties in 1788. In 1803, Dumfries was supplanted by the establishment of a district court in Haymarket, as Haymarket was nearer to the middle of the district.

The Act of Religious Toleration (1786) eliminated the requirement for an official state church and enabled the first Methodist Church to be erected at Sudley in 1822. Other denominations, such as the Baptists at Occoquan Church, had representation in the area also. At the onset of the nineteenth century, the county claimed a total population of 12,733 on the 1800 census.

The Bristoe Tract in Prince William County, Virginia, has had a very unique history. It was originally part of the Brent Town Tract, a tract of thirty thousand acres in then Stafford County, Virginia.

The area called Brenton or Brent's Town was originally granted for the purpose of establishing a settlement without religious restrictions. It was part of the original 1669 Charles II grant for the entire Northern Neck extending westward to the Blue Ridge Mountains between the Potomac and the Rappahannock rivers. The initial plan was to attract Catholics and French Huguenots to the area. The owners would pay thirteen shillings and four pence at Jamestown annually on St. John the Baptist Day. Thomas Lord Culpeper granted part of the Brent Town Tract to George Brent, a Catholic, and Richard Foote, Nicholas Hayward, and Robert Bristow, all Protestants, in 1686/7. When the men failed to attract enough religious dissenters, the grant passed into the hands of Lord Culpeper. Ultimately, London merchants obtained the land and chose Brent to head the settlement since he lived there. William Fitzhugh served as Culpeper's attorney, and all the partners received generous grants within the many acres involved.

The tract was surveyed and divided in 1737 with Robert Bristow, the heir of the original grantee, receiving seventy-five hundred acres between Kettle Run and Broad Run that included the present-day town of Brentsville.

Chapter II

The Development of Western Prince William County

1800–1860

The nineteenth century opened with the highly contentious presidential election of Thomas Jefferson that led to the adoption of the Twelfth Amendment to the U.S. Constitution separating elections of the president and vice president. Several events in Jefferson's administration impacted Prince William County. The 1803 Louisiana Purchase, followed by the expeditions of Lewis and Clark, siphoned off residents to points west of the Bull Run Mountains and to the

The seat of Prince William County was moved from Dumfries to Brentsville in 1820. The Brentsville Courthouse and jail were built in 1821 on land granted from the Brent tract located at the geographic center of the county. (Courtesy of Prince William County, Virginia, Department of Public Works, Historic Preservation Division)

Shenandoah Valley. Census records indicated the county's population dropped in 1810 to 11,111 and continued to drop to a low of 7,504 in 1870. The national Embargo Act, followed by the declaration of war against Great Britain in 1812, held shipping at an impasse. In 1814, enemy ships were anchored in the Potomac River off present-day Quantico. The citizens of Dumfries, in fear of being attacked, activated county vigilantes, but a terrible gale saved the town from the same destructive fate as was suffered by the nation's capital.

At the war's end in 1815, fifth- and sixth-generation descendants of early Virginia settlers moved into western Prince William County. This shifting settlement pattern led to a transfer of the courthouse from Dumfries to Brentsville, considered the midpoint of the county in 1822.

Before 1800, early attempts to cultivate tobacco as a staple quickly proved futile as Northern Piedmont Virginia land was unsuitable. Therefore, plantation owners changed predominately

Liberia Plantation, also known as the Brick House, was built by King Carter's granddaughter, Harriet Bladen Mitchell, and her husband, William J. Weir, in 1825.

Tempers flared and abusive language rang out during a political dispute between James Kempe of Birmingham Green, an ardent Republican, and Bernard Hooe of Wilcoxon, an ardent Federalist. Hooe struck Kempe with a riding whip, whereupon a stronger Kempe thrashed him. Hooe challenged Kempe to a duel on Friday, October 13, 1809. Since dueling was illegal and heavily punished in Virginia, they met across the Potomac in Maryland, each with their seconds and surgeons. Kempe sustained a slight wound to his leg while Hooe fell mortally wounded. Taken by rowboat to Rippon Lodge near present-day Woodbridge, Hooe died the following day. Before the year was over, Kempe, his wife, and five-year-old daughter Margaret moved to Mississippi. Margaret would become the mother of Varina Howell Davis, First Lady of the Confederacy.

Birmingham Green as it appeared in the 1950s near Route 28/Centreville Road. The structure was demolished in the 1980s to build the Manassas Shopping Center.

to corn and wheat as their main staples. The majority of plantations established before the Civil War were "middling," of about one thousand acres, insufficient acreage to support tobacco cultivation. Slave help ranged from as few as two or three people on the smaller plantations to upwards of one hundred, depending on the size and type of work on the sites. Additionally, many planters raised cattle, sheep, and swine for diary products, wool, and food. Grantees receiving land were expected to build houses and suitable dependencies, cultivate staple crops, and plant fruit trees where feasible.

In addition to his Northern Neck plantation, Corotoman, Robert "King" Carter initially had forty-odd smaller plantations managed by overseers. As a Virginia agent, Carter converted one of his warehouses into a land office for these proprietary operations, and he quickly surveyed and sold land tracts earning five hundred pounds (about $100,000 in 2009 dollars) in the first year of his oversight. Ultimately, he gave choice tracts of about one hundred thousand acres to his heirs from this land dynasty. His sons, Robert II, who received the Lower Bull Run tract, and Landon II, who received the Middle Bull Run tract, in turn, subdivided their tracts to their children and grandchildren.

In the Lower Bull Run tract named Libra, 2,860 acres were inherited by Robert III's daughter Priscilla Carter Mitchell. She then gave 1,660 acres of this tract to her daughter Harriet Bladen Mitchell, who married William James Weir. The Weirs built their brick home, Liberia, in 1825. Weir became one of the more prosperous entrepreneurs in the area. He served as a lawyer and had a store in

Centreville from 1818 to 1825. The Weirs established a small community on the plantation along the road to Centreville, which included a dry goods store selling groceries and produce (the only store of its sort between Centreville and Brentsville) and a post office. Weir was postmaster from 1829 to 1852. Toward mid-century, he opened Liberia Academy, a school for boys from well-to-do families, offering a classical education. He operated a blacksmith shop and maintained a mill and a warehouse.

At its peak right before the outbreak of the Civil War in 1861, Liberia was Prince William County's largest and wealthiest plantation, worked by ninety slaves.

By the 1820s, middling plantations were scattered from New Market/Centreville in the north past the Bull Run and into the area of current Manassas City. In 1801, James Kempe and his wife Margaret Bird purchased Birmingham Green, situated on present-day Route 28/Centreville Road two and a quarter miles east of Liberia Plantation. Kempe was one of the first newspaper publishers in the county and was affiliated with the *Republican Journal* and the *Dumfries Advertiser.*

In the 1820s, this property came into the ownership of the Kincheloe family. Southeast several miles was Mayfield, the family home of Robert H. Hooe, who owned hundreds of acres in the area of present-day Manassas. About two miles southwest of Birmingham Green was Clover Hill. Purchased by Rutt Johnson, a native of New Jersey, in 1770 from Patrick Hamrick, the plantation grew from an initial 130 to more than 1,500 acres. Working to replenish land depleted by tobacco, father and sons planted wheat, oats, hay, and orchards of apples and peaches. Soon the land was home to sheep, cows, buffalo, oxen, hogs, horses, and many new oak trees.

Down the road southeast from Clover Hill were Moor Green, the home of James Hooe, and Bloom Hill, the home of the Cockrell family. Another neighbor was John Lee of Willow Green on Balls Ford Road where a later owner, William Wheeler, made apple brandy in a two and one-half story distillery.

During these years, land bordering the dirt path called Sudley Road leading west toward Young's Branch of the Bull Run, was settled by other Carter descendents. The whole region was originally known as the Middle Bull Run Tract patented to King Carter's son Landon I. In turn, Landon I split the land between his sons, Landon II and John. In 1832, Benjamin Tasker Chinn had the 750-acre Ben Lomond Plantation about a mile from the Warrenton Turnpike/Route 29 on land deeded through his mother, Sarah Fairfax Carter. The plantation spanned both sides of the Bull Run. North of the Warrenton Pike along Sudley Road was Pittsylvania, the home of Landon Carter II. In 1851, a portion of this site was sold to Alfred Ball, who also bought the grand mansion Portici from Spencer

Ben Lomond plantation house on Sudley Manor Drive was built in 1832 by Benjamin Tasker Chinn on land from the Cancer Tract deeded to him from his mother, Sarah Fairfax Carter. (Courtesy of Daniel G. Tassa)

Ball. John built Sudley Plantation to the north of the Warrenton Pike. Both sons were living on their plantations when the First Battle of Manassas (Bull Run) occurred.

Other homes in the vicinity of Sudley Road included Benjamin Chinn's Hazel Plain, John Dogan's Rosefield, and Judith Carter Henry's Spring Hill, all properties now in the boundaries of the Manassas National Battlefield Park. As the nineteenth century progressed, these landowners developed a community of mutual interest around agricultural production. John Carter oversaw construction of Sudley Mill, area families built the Sudley Methodist Church, and the Warrenton Turnpike expanded west to Gainesville and Warrenton. Taverns similar to the Stone House appeared on the turnpike and along Route 28/Centreville Road. By mid-nineteenth century, visitors came to the modest Sudley Springs Hotel for the "waters." The area became a vacation site and summer resort for people from throughout Virginia and as far away as Louisiana and Mississippi. With completion of the Manassas Gap Railroad in 1852, local families and tourists could travel to the new station in Gainesville. Within a half-hour, a wagon carried visitors the five-mile distance from the station to the hotel. Weekly accommodations at the popular destination were $5.00 for adults and $2.50 for children.

Sudley Springs Hotel, pictured here in the 1890s, attracted visitors on vacation who came for the "waters," arriving from throughout Virginia and as far away as Louisiana. The Sudley Sulfur Spring House was destroyed in the Civil War.

In an unusual move for his time, Robert "Councillor" Carter III of the Northern Neck gave all of his land away in 1791 and freed his five hundred slaves. Some of the freed slaves moved into the "Thoroughfare" area of western Prince William County, where their direct descendants continue to live. Some surnames are Gaskins and Harris. The descendants of another free black, Robert Nickens, of Lancaster County, Pennsylvania, also migrated there. Most of the farmers in the Lower Bull Run tract relied upon slave labor to cultivate crops and upon the Warrenton Turnpike to transport their agricultural products to markets further east.

Slave quarters on the Ben Lomond plantation. (Courtesy of Daniel G. Tassa)

In 1800, there were 5,416 slaves in the county or 43 percent of the population. The interdependency of slave labor and white overseers made the local economy run. Grain production was seasonal and, unlike tobacco, required fewer laborers to produce it. When grains replaced tobacco as the main crops for these planters, it forced them to develop more efficient use of their slaves. Slaves slowly became extensions of planters' hands by working at all aspects of farming. In addition, slaves became adept at skilled trades such as carpentry, stone masonry, milling, and dairying, while continuing to plant and harvest crops. Larger planters with more slaves found it feasible to rent out some of their slaves during harvests. Others found it best to employ their female slaves in plantation industries such as spinning wool or cultivating, spinning, and weaving flax to make linen for plantation use or to sell to local stores.

By 1860, 28 percent of the population, or 2,356 people, were enslaved in Prince William County. In 1860, William James Weir of Liberia Plantation was the largest slaveholder, holding ninety slaves. John and Frances Gibson of Fleetwood near

Chapman's (Beverley) Mill at Thoroughfare Gap, built in 1742, was a busy operation that processed wheat and corn from farms in the area. In July 1861, the Confederates turned the mill into a meat-curing warehouse and distribution center for cattle and pigs to supply the army. Although the Confederates burned the mill in 1862, the Beverly family restored the operation and had it running again by 1876.

This 1890s photograph shows the original Robinson house (the middle section) with additions, built in 1840 by James "Gentleman Jim" Robinson (1799–1875), a free African American. Before the Civil War, Robinson bought his wife, Susan Gaskins, and all of his children except two sons. Unfortunately, these sons were sold to New Orleans when their owner, Landon Carter, needed cash. Only one returned home after the war was over. The site is now within the boundaries of the Manassas National Battlefield Park.

Brentsville and Edmund Berkeley of Evergreen each owned fifty-two slaves. Of the black population in Piedmont Prince William, the number of freed individuals tripled during these years. Many of them bought their own land and stayed in the county to be near their still-enslaved family members.

By the 1850s, some plantation families, faced with mounting debt and a proliferation of heirs, were forced to sell or free their slaves. Slave auctions were a feature of everyday life in the area, occurring at community gathering places in Haymarket, Brentsville, and Newgate (Centreville area). W. R. Millan, a major slave trader, frequented the Prince William Courthouse in Brentsville in search of slaves to sell at high prices in New Orleans. Runaways were advertised statewide.

Upon learning that he was about to be sold by his master, James A. Carter of Prince William County, the slave James M. Peters escaped and enrolled for three years in Company E, First U.S. Colored Infantry, which was assigned to the Department of Virginia and North Carolina, General Benjamin Butler's Army of the James. After the war, Peters returned to his mother's home in Prince William County, took up farming, and raised a family of ten children.

Throughout Virginia, the number of free blacks mounted. Some owners made a profit by hiring their slaves out for added income, while others allowed some of their slaves to keep enough earnings to buy their own freedom. Such was the situation of James "Gentleman Jim" Robinson in 1840. Formerly owned by Landon Carter II, who fathered him with a slave woman, Robinson bought his freedom and four acres of land on the Warrenton Pike. Over time, he accumulated 170 more acres, married a white English immigrant servant, and had six children, most of whom he eventually bought from Carter. Two of his sons, still enslaved at the beginning of the Civil War, were sent to New Orleans where their stone masonry skills went for a high price: only one son returned. Following the war, Robinson rebuilt his home and accumulated an additional 1,500 acres of land between Sudley Road and Newgate and ran a tavern on the pike. His home was engulfed in both battles of Manassas, allowing him to make a sizeable claim for losses from the U.S. government after the war.

The headstone of James "Gentleman Jim" Robinson placed near his home.

By 1827, two stagecoach lines a week ran between Alexandria and the Orange County courthouse, with a stop at Gainesville on the Warrenton-Alexandria Turnpike. The route quickly gained passenger as well as commercial traffic, carrying local products by

ORANGE & ALEXANDRIA R. R.

Only Safe and Certain Line!

NO DETENTION FROM ICE!!

Omnibuses leave Washington City, at 6 o'clock, A. M., on the arrival of the Cars from *Baltimore*, to convey Passengers to *Alexandria*, where they can *Breakfast*, and take the Cars of the *Orange & Alexandria Rail-road*, and arrive at *Gordonsville* by 11 o'clock.

The Trains of the *Virginia Central Rail-road* connect at *Gordonsville*, and will convey Passengers to *Richmond*, *Charlottesville* and *Staunton*; reaching the former place by half-past 2 o'clock, in time to connect with all the Lines going South and West.

W. B. BROCKETT,
Agent.

December, 8th, 1854.

Orange & Alexandria Railroad advertisement from 1854. This line became part of the double-track main line of the Southern Railway System between Washington, D.C., and the South.

wagon to Alexandria and returning with manufactured goods. In 1849, the Orange & Alexandria Railroad began laying track westward, planning to run to rural Tudor Hall near Manassas. The state General Assembly voted to pay three-fifths of the track cost, and stock subscriptions of $170,000 were sold. Charles Hunton, a wealthy planter and state senator in the area, became one of three original directors with John S. Barbour Jr.

and Charles J. Stover. Barbour, a member of the Virginia House of Delegates, oversaw the railroad first as director, then as president.

Iron for the rails came from England and New York, but lumber for the crossties was supplied by local residents. When many residents balked at railroad demands for free rights-of-way through their property, their cries for compensation delayed progress by six months. Black laborers, predominately slaves, performed most of the line's construction and maintenance. They cut wood, graded the track bed, broke stone for ballast, laid track, and cleared snow. Irish immigrants vied for similar work, but slave labor was cheaper. Blacksmiths, carpenters, and mechanics used their talents in the construction.

By October 1851, several passenger and freight trains passed through Prince William County weekly. The track ran to Lynchburg as a final destination. So successful was it that the General Assembly authorized a second railroad to link the farmers of the Shenandoah Valley with the port of Alexandria. The new Manassas Gap Railroad would run from Harrisonburg to Strasburg through the Blue Ridge Mountains at Manasseh's Gap and on to Tudor Hall to connect with the Orange & Alexandria Railroad. Investors chose Edward Carrington Marshall, the youngest son of U.S. Supreme Court Chief Justice John Marshall, who was worth over $120,000 (about $3.1 million in 2008 dollars), as president. Local planters from western Prince William and Fauquier counties served on the Board of Directors. An agreement with the Orange & Alexandria allowed the Manassas Gap Railroad to rent its tracks from Tudor Hall. In 1853, the Manassas Gap Railroad began service from Strasburg through Manassas Junction, the new name given to Tudor Hall, which was a local plantation, now a mail drop and census site.

Before long, the annual track rental of $33,500 proved too costly. The Manassas Gap decided to lay its own track as an independent line, diverting at Gainesville to pass over the Bull

The origin of the name "Manassas" is undetermined. No one knows for certain how the city of Manassas got its name. Some believe it is a Native American term. General W. H. Payne of Fauquier County, who was known locally in the late 1800s as an authority of Indian nomenclature, surmised that Massanutten Mountain and Manassas Gap had a common Indian origin. Local lore suggests "Manasseh" was the name of a French-Jewish innkeeper in the Shenandoah Valley near Manassas Gap. Those familiar with the Old Testament argue it is a biblical reference to two kings named Manasseh. Dr. Raus Hanson of Madison College must have favored this legend because, in his study of the meaning of Virginia place names, he simply entered "from Manasseh's" as the origin of Manassas.

Historian Eugene Scheel tells us that first settlers of the late 1720s through the 1740s gave the name "Manassas Gap" (with various spellings) to the corridor's broad entrance at Linden. Manassas is an Indian word meaning "basket shaped," reflective of the broad curving gap.

Little concrete evidence exists to support any one theory.

Run near Sudley Church, crossing Cub Run, past the Chantilly Post Office across Little River Turnpike, and past Fairfax Courthouse to Alexandria. The railroad purchased an eighty-foot-wide right-of-way along the proposed route in 1854 and began construction. Slaves and Irish laborers felled trees and cleared the path. Work gangs made the cuts and fills. When some slaves rioted, cavalry captain Turner Ashby of Harrisonburg and his company were called in to quell it.

Unfortunately, the railroad ran out of money in 1858 and suspended operations. Although the Manassas Gap never completed its second line, the two railroads altered the landscape and lifestyle of the local populace forever, spurred economic growth, and encouraged development. Both Sudley and Chapman (later Beverley) mills flourished because of the ability to ship local bumper crops of wheat and corn. In the village now referred to as Manassas Junction or simply "The Junction," William Brawner served as postmaster, railroad agent, and storekeeper. The railroad's presence led to the construction of a boardinghouse, several scattered houses, and a makeshift train depot for the Orange & Alexandria line, the most direct rail route from Washington to Richmond.

Events near and far slowly encroached upon the lives of local residents. John Brown, virulent abolitionist and villain of Pottawatomie Creek, Kansas, led an unsuccessful raid in October 1859 on the arsenal at Harpers Ferry some fifty miles west of Prince William County. Talk of severing the federal union was rampant as voters went to the polls in November 1860. With the election of Abraham Lincoln, seven deep southern states split from the Union and formed the Confederacy, with a capital in Montgomery, Alabama.

In the 1860 presidential election, Virginians cast most of their ballots for candidate John Bell of the Constitutional Union party, which spoke vaguely of adherence to the Constitution, the Union, and the laws of the United States. Virginians waited until February 1861 to convene a secession convention in Richmond. Here much of the discussion centered around the possible influence of Republican patronage within the state and the threat posed for the continuation of slavery. Of the five thousand people in the entire county, nearly half were slaves or freed blacks.

On May 23, 1861, Virginians were asked to accept the Ordinance of Secession passed by a Richmond convention after the fall of Fort Sumter on April 12 and after President Lincoln's follow-up call for seventy-five thousand volunteers to subdue rebellious southerners. In a countywide referendum, Prince William County voted 841 to 38 to support secession from the federal union.

"I cannot raise my hand against my relatives, my children, my home," Robert E. Lee proclaimed once war was declared by Virginia voters in the special statewide referendum vote supporting secession. Immediately, Lee resigned his Federal commission and was appointed general of the Army of Northern Virginia by Confederate President Jefferson Davis. Recognizing the potential for a Federal Army advancement toward the Shenandoah Valley, Virginia's breadbasket, Lee engaged local citizens to scout the terrain of Manassas Junction and vicinity for potential fortifications to protect the intersection of the two railroads. He ordered General Pierre Gustave Toutant Beauregard, the "hero of Fort Sumter," to oversee the buildup of massive fortifications to protect the Junction from Yankee infiltration. Meanwhile, at Arlington Heights, General Lee's home, Federal General Irwin McDowell quickly occupied the plantation, making it his headquarters from which he plotted action at Manassas Junction thirty miles away.

Chapter III

War Changes the Landscape

1860–1865

On June 1, 1861, General P. G. T. Beauregard, leading the Confederate Army of the Potomac, took command of the Manassas area under orders from President Jefferson Davis. Within days, General Beauregard addressed an order to the "Good People" of Prince William, Loudoun and Fairfax counties to send their slaves, numbering over two thousand, to help build earthwork fortifications and trenches. The build-up stretched from Newgate through Union Mills southward to Signal Hill and the Hooe family property (Mayfield) into Manassas around the junction and out to Cannon Branch near the Manassas Airport. Hastily built fortifications included Fort Pickens and Fort Beauregard near William Weir's home Liberia, the site eventually chosen by Beauregard for his headquarters. This gigantic undertaking transformed the landscape around Manassas Junction. Confederate soldiers continued to arrive by rail, the newest form of troop transportation, often to engage in the building efforts, but did not perform the heaviest work; slaves did that.

Confederate General Pierre Gustave Toutant Beauregard (1818–1893), the "Hero of Fort Sumter," used his engineering background to design and build the fortifications at Manassas. (Engraved from a photograph taken in 1865, *The Military Operations of General Beauregard in the War Between the States* by Alfred Roman, 1884, Vol. 1)

When cannon ran short for the higher elevations, they devised "Quaker" guns, decoy cannon carved from felled tree trunks weighing six hundred to seven hundred pounds, painted black and aimed in the direction of the expected enemy. At a great distance, it was impossible to tell the difference. Mayfield was fortified while Signal Hill used flags to signal the enemy's approach, a first for wartime. Defensive works were erected at major crossings of the Bull Run three miles east of the junction. Outposts stretched nearly eight miles along all major roads leading east. In the valley, General Joseph E. Johnston and his eleven-thousand-

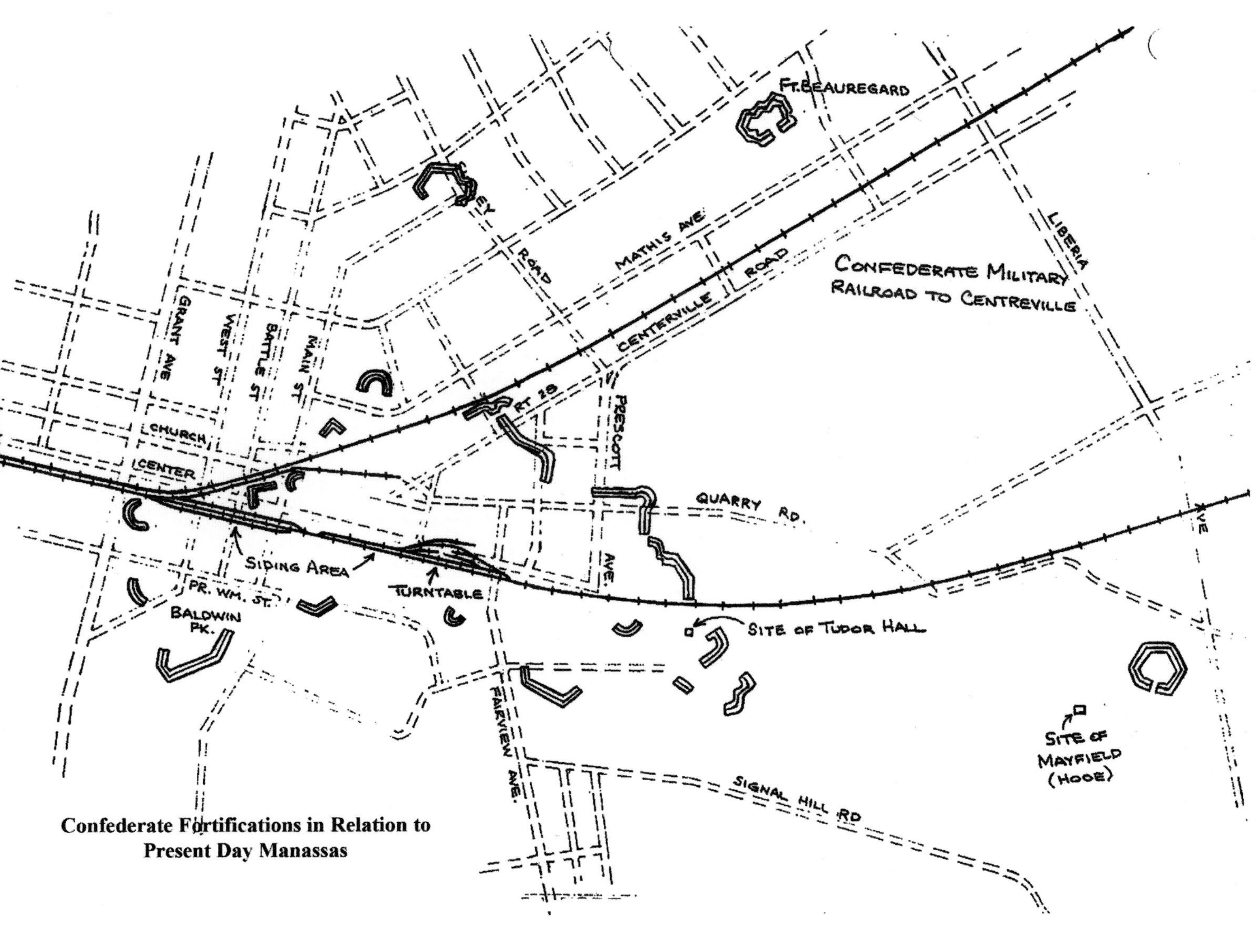

man Army of the Shenandoah was expected to move east as backup once action was imminent. Locally, able-bodied white men, young and old, rallied on several occasions outside of the Brentsville Courthouse to join other county men in the Confederate ranks to defend their homes.

This overlay map of present-day Manassas indicates Confederate earthwork fortifications constructed prior to the First Battle of Manassas relative to Manassas streets. (After a map provided by Van Loan Naiswald)

This sketch depicts a fake "Quaker" gun, used to make the enemy think Confederate fortifications were stronger than they were. Finally, after the Confederates left the area in March 1862, Federal troops and reporters saw for themselves the famous defenses, nicknamed "Monster Manassas." Reactions were mixed. Some say the defenses would not have held before a "determined and vigorous siege" (*Utica Morning Herald*). Union officer George F. McFarland said they "excelled for natural adaptation to defense."

General Joseph Eggleston Johnston's (1807–1891) fresh reinforcements from the Shenandoah Valley arrived at Manassas in time to help Beauregard turn the tide in First Battle of Manassas. Johnston stayed at Manassas Junction until March 1862. (Engraved from a photograph taken in 1867, *The Military Operations of General Beauregard in the War Between the States* by Alfred Roman, 1884, Vol. 1)

As early as July 18, 1861, life for the Frank Lewis family of Portici Plantation changed irrevocably. A skirmish at Blackburn's Ford close to Wilmer McLean's home, Yorkshire, forced the Lewises to abandon their home, Portici, for Fannie Lewis's former home, Snow Hill, located northwest of Route 234 and Route 15. Before reaching Snow Hill, a very pregnant Fannie delivered her fourth child along the Warrenton Turnpike. The sweeping view of the Bull Run landscape from Portici led Confederate Joseph E. Johnston to occupy it as his command post upon arriving in the area just as the first battle began.

Meanwhile, General Beauregard, dining with Wilbur McLean at Yorkshire, watched as a spent cannon ball landed in the fireplace.

The Fourth Virginia Cavalry, Confederate States of America, was organized as a militia in the winter of 1858–59 during the John Brown Raid (locally known as the "excitement") at Harpers Ferry. They drilled monthly at Brentsville. The Prince William Cavalry flag was made by the Misses Emma (later Mrs. Lucian A. Davis) and Sommerville Williams, cousins, and presented to the cavalry at a picnic held at Hart's Woods (near Bristow) in the summer of 1859. The Virginia Seal painted on the flag was signed "Jefferies 186_." Thomas Jefferies was a Baltimore sign and banner painter who converted a U.S. militia flag to the "Stars and Bars" pattern in 1861. The eleven stars represented the eleven Confederate states. The cavalry went into service April 7, 1861, carrying the Prince William Cavalry flag.

In 1861, George Washington's will was removed from Fairfax Courthouse by Alfred Moss, clerk of the court, for safekeeping after Virginia seceded from the federal union. It was kept safe by Mrs. John Brent Hunton, Moss's daughter, at Evergreen Farm, halfway between New Baltimore and Warrenton. The will was placed in a chest containing family silver, buried in the wine cellar, and covered with coal. Moss was arrested and confined to the Old Capitol Prison in Washington City. Once released, Moss went to Evergreen, retrieved the will, and took it with other valuable papers to the Confederate capital in Richmond for safekeeping until the hostilities ended. In 1865, the will was returned to the courthouse.

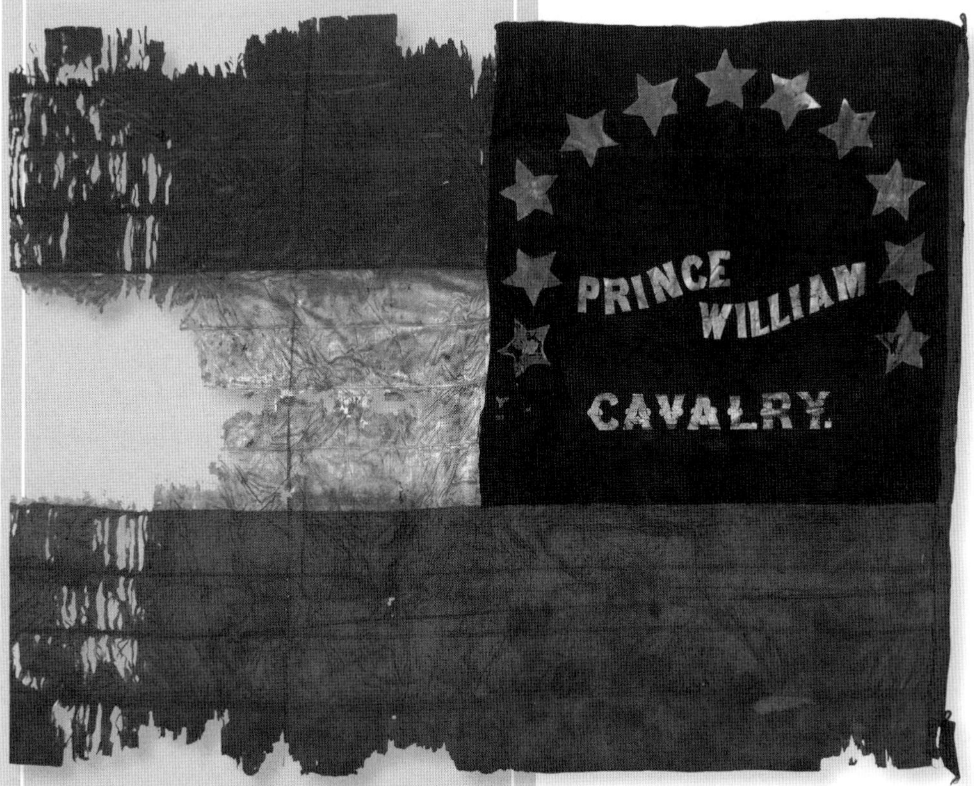

Prince William Cavalry flag. Militia flag of Company A, Fourth Virginia Cavalry, Confederate States of America. (Courtesy of Howard L. Churchill)

Portici, a prosperous middling plantation, the home of Francis Ware Lewis (1822–1913), was the headquarters of General Joseph E. Johnston during the First Battle of Manassas. The house was used as a field hospital after First Manassas and burned to the ground after the Second Battle of Manassas in 1862. The site is now located in the Manassas National Battlefield Park.

Quickly, Beauregard left and eventually established his permanent headquarters at Liberia Plantation.

Sunday morning, July 21, 1861, dawned sunny and bright. During the previous night, the first men of the Union Army approached the Centreville/Newgate area after a relatively peaceful march out of Washington City. They camped overnight at Centreville after leisurely making a three-day march westward from Washington. Despite orders to close ranks, it was not unusual for many men to casually wander off

THE SUDLEY SPRINGS ROAD
Looking toward Sudley Springs from the slope of the Henry House hill

The Sudley Springs Road (Route 622 or Featherbed Lane) looking toward Sudley Springs from the slope of the Henry House saw troop movements and action during the early Civil War. (*Battles and Leaders of the Civil War*, Vol. 1, N.Y., Century Company, 1887)

First Sudley Church - March 1862. Stone Fireplace was probably erected by soldiers during the First Battle of Manassas.

In 1822, Landon Carter II of Woodland, great-grandson of Robert "King" Carter, donated three-quarters of an acre of land to build the Sudley Church. This first church building was erected sometime between 1822 and the early 1840s. Services were held by circuit riders and lay leaders. During the Civil War, Sudley Church was used as a military hospital in July 1861 during the First Battle of Manassas and in August 1862 during Second Manassas. This first church building was razed because of damage received during these battles. March 1862 photograph. (Library of Congress)

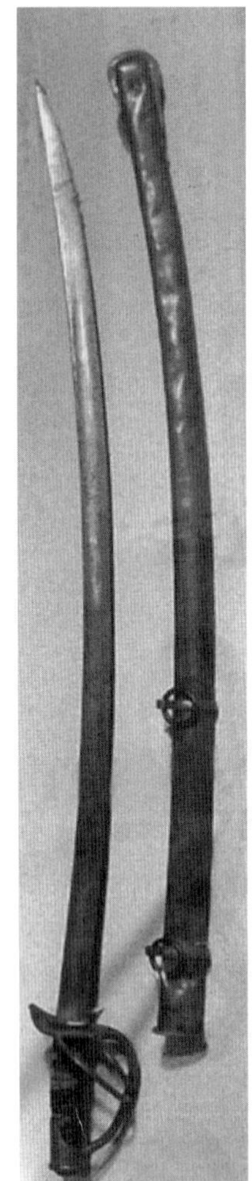

and pick the wild berries growing by the roadside. General Irvin McDowell decided to skirt the formidable fortifications built by the Confederates and attack them upstream toward Sudley Church. Crossing Cub Run on a suspension bridge, he led his men overland to the narrow double-arched stone bridge, leaving a small contingent of men at that location. At some point during this final march, he connected with a local man of uncertain name who led the army around the Confederate left flank two to three miles above Stone Bridge to Sudley Ford. Meanwhile, General Beauregard was alerted by a message sent to him by telegraph from Confederate spy Rose Greenhow in Washington revealing when the Union

Amos Benson with his saber. The Confederacy copied the U.S. Model 1860 Light Cavalry saber with a three-branch cast brass guard and steel scabbard. It has a leather-wrapped grip with a brass retaining wire. Confederate factories produced sabers closely modeled on this design but may have substituted materials when the correct ones were not available.

Although Amos Benson is known for his Confederate service with Company A, Fourth Virginia (Prince William) Cavalry, history also remembers Benson and his wife Margaret for an act of kindness to a wounded Union soldier that was repaid years after the war.

Late in the afternoon of July 21, 1861, John L. Rice of the Second New Hampshire had a bullet rip into his body as he and his comrades made one last attempt to dislodge Confederates on Henry Hill. In retreat, comrades carried him off the field to an area near Sudley Church where Union surgeons were working. Under fear of attack by Confederate cavalry, they left Rice, who appeared dead, at a nearby fence.

Amos Benson found Rice, stripped away his bloody clothing, cleaned out the vermin that had tormented him, and constructed a crude tent around him. After ten days of care, Rice had improved enough to be moved to Sudley Church, then used as a hospital, and eventually recovered from his wounds. Later, he was well enough to be transported to Libby Prison in Richmond from which he was exchanged and served again.

In 1886, Rice made his way back from New Hampshire to the Benson home inquiring how he might repay them for saving his life. The Bensons asked for help to repay the $200 debt still owed on the rebuilt Sudley Church. Rice returned home, advertised an appeal in local newspapers, and sent the Bensons a thank-you check of $235.

Army would arrive. This information allowed him to establish a favorable position along the Bull Run, forcing Union forces to attack, which they did. Flag signals alerted him to arriving troops early that morning.

The Chinn House as it appeared after First Manassas. Built on a rise, the house was in the center of the field of battle in August 1862.

Imagine the amazement of the Dogan family of the Groveton area who were walking to services at Sudley Church when they saw Union soldiers crossing the ford. Twelve-year-old Molly Dogan's memory, still vivid years later, recalled seeing the soldier's sabers glistening in the sunlight. Around 9:00 a.m., other residents of the area, dressed in their Sunday finery, began making their way to church but soon turned around. A crowd of worshipers already at the church quickly dispersed when echoes of gunfire from Union officer Ambrose Burnside's men opened up on a Confederate brigade further down the dirt road. Nannie Leachman Carroll reported that, as a young woman, her "Mama said it was a terrible day." Nannie's home, Woodville, about a mile from the main battle, was hit by cannon balls throughout the day. Nannie remembers that she and her four siblings huddled under a large sideboard during the prolonged battle until the firing ceased at night. Then her mother ventured outside and saw their yard covered with dead and dying soldiers of both sides. Later, Mrs. Leachman helped bury elderly Judith Carter Henry, who refused to leave her home and was the only civilian killed in the battle. In the Newgate area, eleven-year-old Belle J. Holden said that when the battle began, "the house shook and trembled; the darkies rushed from their cabins panic-stricken to hide behind a big cliff at the back of the farm." Level Green, her home, became a hospital for wounded at battle's end.

Brigadier General Eppa Hunton (1822–1908), former school teacher and lawyer, played an active role in democratic politics. At the outbreak of the Civil War, he was serving as commonwealth attorney at Brentsville. He was elected to the Virginia Secession Convention, and when the convention voted to secede on April 17, 1861, he immediately applied for a commission in the Virginia forces. Governor John Letcher commissioned him colonel of the Eighth Regiment Virginia Infantry, which earned the name "the Bloody Eighth." In this 1863 photograph, he is around forty years old.

First Manassas (Bull Run) was a Confederate victory, yet both armies were "green" and untested. Here, Thomas J. Jackson, a thirty-seven-year-old former instructor at the Virginia Military Institute, became immortalized as the great "Stonewall" who led his troops uphill to victory. Here, Union officer William T. Sherman. whose men marked the war's end, got his first taste of bloodshed. Here, young men, northerners and southerners, aged enough to realize war killed and was not pleasant. Here for miles, the landscape was covered with bodies strung haphazardly, some living, some dead. The local

Telegram from President Jefferson Davis, C.S.A., to General Samuel Cooper, a close friend of Davis, following First Manassas:

Night has closed upon a hard fought field—Our forces have won a glorious victory. The enemy was routed & fled precipatately (sp) abandoning a very large amount of arms, munitions, Knapsacks and Baggige (sp). The Ground was strewn for miles with those Killed & the farm houses and Grounds around were filled with his wounded. The Pursuit was continued along several routes towards Leesburg & Centerville until darkness covered the fugitives. We have captured several field Batteries & Regimental Standards & one US Flag. Many prisoners have been taken—Too high praise cannot be bestowed whether for the skill of the principal officers or for the Gallantry of all the Troops—The Battle was mainly fought on our left, several miles from our field works; a force engaged there not Exceeding Fifteen thousand (15,000) that of the Enemy Estimated at Thirty-five thousand (35,000).

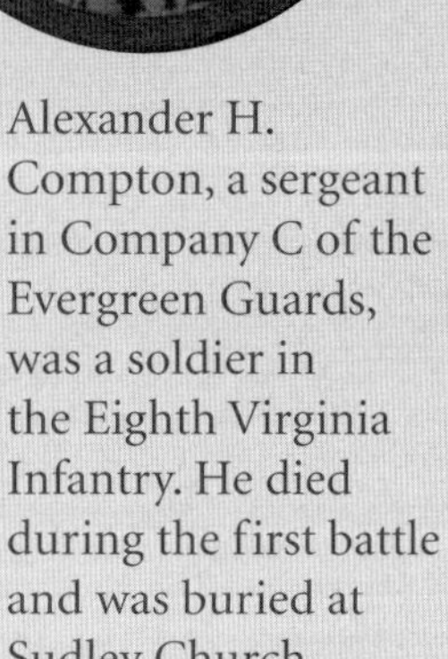

Alexander H. Compton, a sergeant in Company C of the Evergreen Guards, was a soldier in the Eighth Virginia Infantry. He died during the first battle and was buried at Sudley Church.

This sketch details the battlefield after the First Battle of Manassas. From *Battles and Leaders of the Civil War*, Vol. 1. (The Library of Virginia)

population arose miraculously to the tragic circumstances surrounding them to care for the injured and to eventually bury the dead. Wagons hauled the wounded to Sudley Church, the Stone House, and Portici, each serving as a makeshift hospital. Wounded were carried into other private homes still standing near the battlefield. Other wounded of both sides were carried to homes and churches from Manassas Junction to Fairfax. Still others were placed on rail cars to be taken to Richmond for care or incarceration. Approximately nine hundred men were killed that day while twenty-seven hundred were wounded.

Because of the Washington visitors who had come out to watch the action, Union forces were hampered in their retreat from the field of battle. Most thought the battle would be an easy Union victory and did not expect to be caught in a desperate Union rout. Civilians with picnic baskets, carriages, and unstable horses added to the confusion, extending the retreat for days as everyone staggered back to Washington.

In August 1862, Confederate General Robert E. Lee ordered General Thomas J. "Stonewall" Jackson to keep General John Pope's and General George B. McClellan's Union armies from uniting. Jackson captured Bristoe Station and Manassas Junction late on August 26. When reports reached Pope, he thought it was one of General J.E.B. Stuart's raids and ordered General George W. Taylor's infantry brigade to drive the imagined cavalrymen away. Meanwhile, about 6:00 a.m. on August 27, Colonel Gustav Waagner led the Second New York Heavy Artillery from nearby Bull Run to engage Jackson northeast of Liberia Plantation house. Jackson quickly counterattacked and sent the New Yorkers retreating to Centreville. When Taylor's command arrived about 8:30 as Waagner began withdrawing, Jackson's men, entrenched in a line between Liberia and Fort Mayfield, prepared to greet it with a "storm of lead." The Federals advanced within three hundred yards of Fort Beauregard, and Jackson rode forward waving a white handkerchief to suggest they surrender. When a Union bullet flew past Jackson's head, he ordered his troops to open fire. Taylor fell mortally wounded, and his force retreated to the Orange & Alexandria Railroad and the Bull Run Bridge.

Meanwhile, cheers of victory were heard from the Confederates, especially after President Jefferson Davis came on the field to greet them, walking through a gentle rain. In the days that followed, relatives of both sides searched for wounded kin while mass graves were prepared for the dead, blending Union and Confederate men together. So shallow were these graves that farmers would continue to dig up skeletal remains and parts of uniforms and military materials for decades.

One such battle experience was truly enough, but Manassas experienced a rerun on August 28, 1862, in nearly the same locale. General Irvin McDowell made Liberia Plantation his headquarters following Beauregard's abandonment. The Union buildup ultimately attracted the attention of General Stonewall Jackson, however, who led a surprise raid on the facility and some unguarded railroad cars at night. After allowing his men to take whatever they could carry, the building was torched. That drew the attention of Union forces, and a skirmish ensued. Jackson quickly withdrew beyond the junction. Shortly thereafter, the Second Battle of Manassas occurred with similar results as the first. Union forces once again retreated toward Washington. General Robert E. Lee used the victory as a springboard to invade Maryland in September 1862 with disastrous results for the Confederacy. From July 1861 through March 1862, Confederates encamped at Blooms in today's Manassas Park, and at Centreville, connecting Manassas Junction with Centreville by means of the world's first military railroad. When word reached Centreville that U.S. General George McClellan had moved his army to the peninsula in Tidewater Virginia, the Confederates evacuated the Manassas area, allowing the Federals to occupy what was left of the Junction.

As an occupying force in hostile territory, the Union Army faced the task of keeping the supply lines and communications open against raids and sabotage. Guerilla units such as Colonel John Singleton Mosby's Rangers struck hard and often at the railroad. To secure the area, in the fall of 1862, Union General George G. Meade ordered construction of a series of small earthworks along the railroad to guard against guerilla raids. The location of Cannon Branch Fort indicates that it was one of the earthworks built under Meade's orders. It is positioned at the point where the Orange & Alexandria Railroad crossed a stream known as Cannon Branch. The size of the fort suggests it would have held a company of Federal troops and perhaps several cannon. Unlike Mayfield Fort, the Cannon Branch earthwork was not intended to repel an assault but to protect a vital supply line from attacks by small, irregular units.

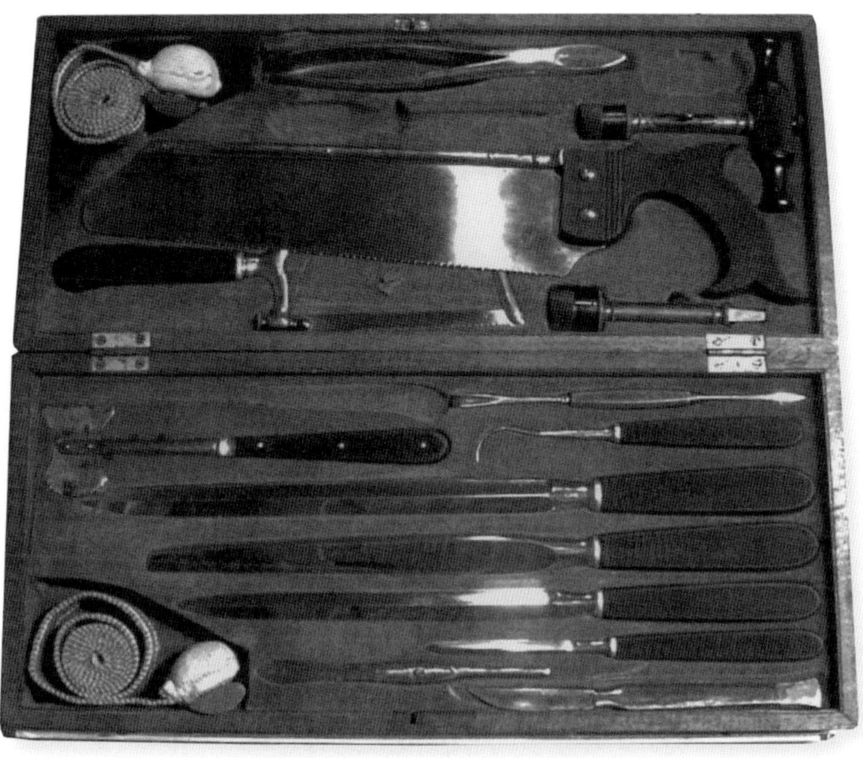

A Civil War field surgeon's kit containing clamps, a variety of probes, a brush, saws, knives, and other medical tools that would have been used by doctors at Sudley Church.

President Lincoln used the Union victory at Antietam as reason to issue his Emancipation Proclamation freeing the slaves in all areas under federal control effective January 1, 1863.

One final flourish of gunfire occurred at Bristoe Station in October 1863 when U.S. General George Meade was marching troops through this area on his way to a federal supply base in Centreville. Confederate Lieutenant General A. P. Hill spotted them and reported the sighting to General Robert E. Lee. Lee ordered an attack without reconnaissance. Meade's artillery pounded the Confederates, resulting in their retreat, giving the Union its only successful northern victory in this area. Despite the ongoing movement of troops through Northern Virginia, for western Prince William County, the war was essentially over. The county was occupied by Union troops for the remainder of the war. They maintained the railroads between Alexandria and Mitchell's Station in Culpeper.

Day Dress, 1850s. This two-piece silk dress is a classic example of the style of day dresses from the 1850s to about 1863. The skirt is tightly gathered to the pointed waist of the bodice. The bodice has a gathered fan front, and the double-ruffled sleeves are cut in a modified pagoda style. The skirt is very full and would have been worn over a horsehair petticoat or several layers of stiffened linen petticoats. The hoop skirt did not come into fashion until 1856.

The harshness of that war was a daily reminder for the local citizenry as they sought to cope with its reality. Their hearty crops of corn and wheat were destroyed by troops of both armies marching throughout the area. Orchards and fences were torn down and used for firewood. Homes, barns, and outbuildings were damaged or destroyed. Livestock and poultry were taken for rations. Many families left the area; with sons in the service and slaves deserting, there was no one to tend the ruined farms. Wilmer McLean of Yorkshire went to Appomattox only to have the surrender occur in his living room in 1865. In the spring of 1862, William James Weir of Liberia Plantation and his second wife Louisa took twenty-five slaves and moved south to Fluvanna County, which saw little fighting. Weir left some faithful slaves, most likely Samuel and Nelly Naylor, at Liberia to care for it. They were given twelve acres of land after the war for their service. Their son Cornelius helped Weir's son Robert Carter Weir run his newly purchased Sudley Mill eight miles away. While Liberia itself suffered little damage despite its use as military headquarters and a hospital, the fields and outbuildings were in shambles. Weir stayed in Fluvanna and died at age seventy-five while visiting Liberia. He is buried in the family plot.

A post-battle camp within the ruins of the Henry House after the First Battle of Manassas, July 1861. Judith Henry, an aged resident who refused to leave her home, was the only civilian killed in this battle. She died in her bed when the center of fighting surged over her property.

To ride out the war, the Johnson family of Clover Hill went to Texas by wagon, driven by their slave Chapman, who was strong and over six feet tall. Upon their return, they discovered their house and crops burnt to the ground by retreating Yankees. Only a craft house and a slave quarter, both built of stone, survived. The family lived in the craft house while their newly freed slaves helped them rebuild their house. Although it was financially difficult, the former slave Chapman ultimately purchased ten acres adjoining the plantation, built a log cabin and moved there, helping found the hamlet of Lucasville, named for a former slave, Lucas. The harshness of the war remained a daily reminder to local citizens.

"We heard of Lee's surrender with distress and incredulity. It seemed too bad to be true," said Eleanor Ewell of Dunblane. For African Americans, however, the reaction was reason for jubilation. Many returning soldiers, permanently disabled by their war experiences, were forced to sell off land or diversify their agricultural activities. Landon Carter's son Edwin was so distraught upon discovering the ruins of Pittsylvania that he never rebuilt the house and lived out his life in a log cabin with his two sisters. A Pennsylvania minister traveling through Manassas Junction

A pontoon bridge built over the Bull Run at Blackburn's Ford to facilitate troop movement in 1862. Matthew Brady photograph. (National Archives)

by train in 1866 observed a "dismal and impoverished" countryside. General Oliver Otis Howard, newly appointed commander of the Freedmen's Bureau, wrote in an official report: "The immediate theatre of operations became a tract of deserted and broken up farms." The war cut across social status, economic stratification, and ethnicity. The county was wasted, homes destroyed, families destitute.

Yet life struggled on despite the ever-present shadow of the memory of opposing forces traipsing back and forth through the region. Where once healthy-producing fields were covered with thickets of weeds and briars, members of both the white and black populations helped each other survive. The human suffering that all citizens had endured for four long years of war was impossible to erase.

In 1862, the Brentsville Courthouse was plundered by soldiers who destroyed or carried off the clerk's papers and county seal as souvenirs. County government ceased to function. A congressional law passed on March 3, 1865, establishing the Bureau of Refugees, Freedmen and Abandoned Lands, was of major significance for the South and for western Prince William and Manassas Junction. Better known as the Freedmen's Bureau, the Bureau's meagerly funded mandate was to distribute rations and medical

All the fords on the Bull Run were hotly contested by both sides. Blackburn's Ford was the crossing of Bull Run by Centreville Road between Manassas and Centreville. This sketch titled "Bridge over Bull Run burned by Rebels" is Alfred R. Waud's depiction of the destruction of the Bull Run railroad bridge near the ford. (*Harper's Weekly*, March 29, 1862)

Two African American women thought to be members of the Naylor family remained behind at Liberia to take care of the plantation when the Weirs fled to Fluvanna County in 1862. Following the war, Nellie (seated) was granted 12.5 acres from the Weirs with their "love and affection."

supplies, establish schools for freedmen and help benevolent societies man them; additionally, it was to regulate labor and contracts while serving as custodians of confiscated lands, and oversee the administration of justice involving freedmen. The first person appointed to manage the calamities of Prince William County was a twenty-four-year-old army veteran named Marcus S. Hopkins.

On September 16, 1865, William James Weir of Liberia Plantation in Manassas filed his Amnesty Oath at the Brentsville Courthouse, swearing to support and defend the Constitution of the United States . . . and support all laws with reference to . . . emancipation of slaves. Weir also requested reimbursement for property destroyed and for lost income during the war years.

Weir wrote:

I am a citizen of the State of Virginia for thirty years or upwards, of the County of Prince William, residing on my farm called "Liberia" near Manassas Station, being engaged this time in farming & grazing—I am upwards of seventy years of age, have never sought or held any political office whatever—my sincere desire has been to perpetuate the union of the states so far as it was in my power. I have never been engaged personally with any business connected with the Army. . . . Several years since I emancipated a number of my servants and wished them to make Liberia, in Africa, their home, but they preferred to locate themselves in the City of Washington, where they are now living and doing very well, I have also been favorable to a gradual emancipation of Servants.

My property exceeds in value 20,000 dollars, as assessed in the year 1860, but would not probably reach that sum if valued at this time—having been almost ruined by the depredations of the two Armies, from which I have suffered to a very large amount, say from one to two hundred- thousand dollars in good money—I very respectfully ask that a special amnesty pardon be granted me—With due & proper respect, I am your obedient servant—

Wm J. Weir

On August 7, 1865, court officers sat for the first time after the war's end in the Brentsville Episcopal Church where Allen Howison was elected presiding judge. Agent Hopkins worked closely with these men during his years in the Freedmen's Bureau. Pursuant to federal Reconstruction legislation, a new Virginia Constitution was required. In 1870, the "Underwood Constitution" was adopted and incorporated public education and the thirteenth, fourteenth, and fifteenth amendments of the federal Constitution giving freedom and civil rights to former slaves. The constitution established local county boards of supervisors to replace the court system as the governing body. Once Manassas was incorporated as a town in 1873, it organized a council to manage local affairs but remained under county jurisdiction. Of immediate concern was reconstructing the telegraph lines, funding road and railroad repairs, and installing a new clerk of the court and a justice of the peace to get business started. Secondary was the hearing of amnesty oaths from former Confederate soldiers so they could practice law in the county.

The 1985 Record and Pension Office papers for James M. Peters (1843–1923). Peters was born in Loudoun County, Virginia. He was 5' 7¼" tall with brown eyes and black hair. Upon learning that he was about to be sold by his Prince William County master, he escaped to Washington City and enlisted. He enrolled for three years in Company E, First U.S. Colored Infantry, which was assigned to the Department of Virginia and North Carolina, General Benjamin Butler's Army of the James.

With the elimination of slavery, so desperate for cash were many planters that they sold or gave land to former slaves, changing the dynamics of black-white relationships. James M. Peters, returning from Union service, bought land from the children of his former owner, Landon Carter II. So, too, did Charles Dean. He and his wife Annie were slaves on adjoining properties of the Cushing and Newman families. By buying property, he was able to unite his wife and family of four children. His eldest child, Jennie, was sent to Washington to work at age fourteen in order to help pay off the mortgage. Some former slaves moved to join the free blacks living in Thoroughfare. Here they acquired parts of several plantations, built homes, and established a farming community. Those who remained on plantations with former masters began working for them under Freedmen's Bureau contracts. Other landowners scaled back by selling land to northerners, especially Pennsylvanians who bought at bargain prices. The area struggled to restore agricultural productivity, commercial activity, and railroad viability. New arrivals helped energize their shell-shocked Virginia neighbors. Within the year, the railroad was in working operation enabling commerce to resume between the fertile Shenandoah Valley and Prince William County and the port of Alexandria. Once again, the junction became functional. Former slaveholders worked to reposition themselves politically and economically, while white middling and tenant farmers hoped for a more democratic playing field. Former slaves enjoyed their freedom and independent lifestyles.

Statue of Confederate hero General Thomas J. Jackson on horseback towers over the Henry House Hill at the Manassas National Battlefield Park. The bronze statue by sculptor Joseph Pollia was unveiled in 1940. Mounted atop an eight-foot base of black granite etched with Brigadier General Barnard Bee's immortal phrase, "There Stands Jackson Like a Stone Wall," the stalwart Jackson in the saddle projected the same strength and determination that Americans needed in the perilous days approaching World War II. (Photograph by Rod Shepherd)

The William James Weir family of Liberia had their loyalties to the Confederacy tested frequently. The plantation had the largest number of slaves, eighty, in the county when the war broke out. Eldest son, William Tasker Weir, had moved to Prince George's County, Maryland, where he was almost drafted into the Union army but escaped by moving back to Virginia after supplying a substitute. Robert Carter Weir, who operated nearby Sudley Mill, cared for wounded soldiers in his home following First Manassas. Robert enlisted in the Forty-ninth Infantry Regiment of Virginia in 1863. The home of daughter Julia and her husband Josiah Wilcoxon, Locust Grove, became the signal station or Signal Hill for the Confederacy. Edgar Vaux Weir, twenty-three, the most secessionist in the family, quickly joined up and was a private with Company A of the Fourth Regiment, Virginia Cavalry. Over time, he was captured three times but always managed to return to active duty, ending his service as a captain. William Weir's youngest son, Walter, a College of William and Mary graduate who was attending law school at the University of Virginia, joined the "Southern Guards" in Charlottesville and later Company H of the Forty-ninth Virginia Infantry in July 1861. He served in Kentucky, Tennessee, and Virginia.

Chapter IV

Peace Produces a New Town

1865–1912

Desolation wafted from the landscape of Manassas Junction as the lone Orange & Alexandria train arrived at the makeshift station on July 4, 1865. Charles W. Fitts and his parents disembarked in the early afternoon. Only Liberia Plantation house and a few workmen's shanties were visible. The freshness of the landscape, however, appealed to Fitts' father Summer, a builder. The Fittses returned later to build Eureka House hotel near the railroad tracks, unaware that they were squatters. During construction, the owner of the property, William S. Fewell, arrived. A native of Brentsville, Fewell had inherited the acreage from his uncle Sanford Thurman, but the outbreak of war chased Fewell away to Lynchburg. Upon his return, he became the local railroad agent and realized the future potential of the area.

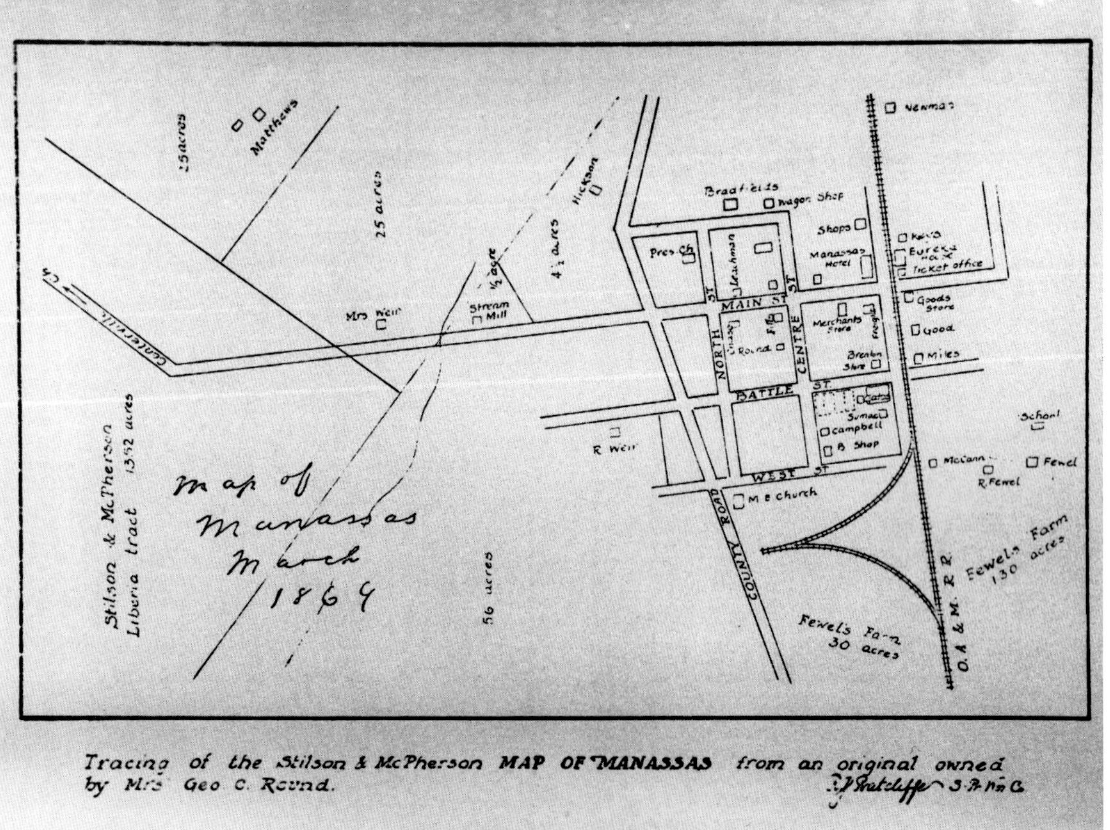

An 1869 map of Manassas, traced by Mrs. George C. Round from an original map by Stilson & McPherson. This shows the town plan. Note that North Street is now called Church Street and the County Road is now Grant Avenue.

Fitts and Fewell came to a mutual and amicable understanding about the land. Fitts built Fewell a house next to the hotel south of the tracks. Between 1867 and 1868, Fewell laid out the town of Manassas on his land and began selling lots running parallel on both sides of the railroad tracks. Within two years, enough lots were sold to fill up several blocks north of the rebuilt depot. At first, Fewell numbered the earliest streets One through Seven going east and west. Running north and south were East, Main, Battle, and West. Once Fewell's lots were developed, they drew others into town, increasing development. Because of the wartime devastation and depopulation, town lots were selling for $2 to $8 an acre ($32.70 to $130.80 in 2009 dollars), making them quite reasonable. George Washington Hixson, who had seen service with Colonel John Mosby's Rangers, was an early purchaser and later became one of the first town council members. He also built the L-shaped Hixson Hall with a woodworking and wheelwright shop with a furniture retail store on the first floor. Exterior stairs led to a sizeable second-floor hall that was used for various meetings.

Fewell's daughter-in-law Sarah became president of the Ladies Memorial Association of Manassas. Following the lead of Mary J. Dogan who had land set aside for the Groveton Confederate Cemetery near the battlefields, Sarah Fewell requested a donated

Top: At 9115 Main Street is a two-story, hip-roofed dwelling that is relatively unchanged since it was built in 1869 or 1870. At that time, it bordered the eastern edge of the Liberia tract. There were only a few houses in the area at the time this residence was built on the bend in what was the old road to Centreville.

Bottom: This pyramidal monument of reddish brown stone, located in the yard of the Henry House at Manassas National Battlefield Park, was erected by Union soldiers in 1865 to the memory of their comrades who fell in the first battle. It is one of the earliest memorial monuments of the Civil War. This photograph might have been taken during the 1911 Manassas National Jubilee of Peace; George Carr Round holds the flag in front.

C. S. Carter's General Store at 9402 Grant Avenue was a favorite place for children from nearby schools to buy penny candy. Carter also advertised "groceries, flour, and feed. I sell groceries and provisions of every kind at lowest prices for first class goods . . . I buy chickens, eggs, and butter and pay the highest market prices for same. Strictly cash or no sale." Still standing on Grant Avenue, the former store now houses offices.

CONFEDERATE MONUMENT,
Unveiled 1889.
Manassas, Virginia.

Above right: The Ladies Memorial Association of Manassas obtained land in the Manassas City Cemetery and funds to build this Confederate monument. Pictured is the 1889 unveiling of the monument in the Manassas Confederate Cemetery, 9117 Center Street.

acre to create a Confederate cemetery in Manassas. The association was interested in memorializing unknown soldiers and their efforts. In 1887, a large obelisk was erected in the Manassas Cemetery to their memory, and over time, numerous unknown soldiers were reinterred there. In 1896, the United Daughters of the Confederacy established a local chapter in Manassas from the Ladies Memorial Association and it continues to this day to maintain graves. In 1916, George Hixson sold 5.16 acres adjacent to the town for a public cemetery.

With the growth of a variety of businesses, the town quickly began to evolve. Hotels, including the Manassas Hotel built on Main Street in the mid-1860s and later called Goodwin House, and Cannon House, built in 1875 by C. E. Brawner, lined the railroad tracks. William C. Merchant opened a store in the Eureka House hotel, starting a family influence lasting into the twenty-first century. The hum of ongoing construction of houses and businesses attracted more residents. Among them was George Carr Round, newly minted graduate of Columbia Law School, New York, who arrived in 1868. Originally headed for North Carolina where he was a Union signal corps officer at war's end, Round disembarked the train to

stretch his legs when it stopped in Manassas. Looking around, he felt the newness, energy, and promise of the hamlet in which he had arrived. Immediately retrieving his luggage, he decided to put his roots down here and take advantage of the town's potential opportunities. By the first of January 1869, he opened his law office and began a flourishing practice, initially based on helping loyal Union farmers in the area make requests for reimbursements on property taken or destroyed by the Union Army. Later he sold real estate.

Round was determined to make worthy contributions to his adopted town. Believing in the importance of education, he supported Freedmen's Bureau efforts to open schools and worked to open the first white public school in Virginia, Ruffner School, in Manassas in 1869. This school was named for Virginia's first public school superintendent, William Ruffner. Shortly thereafter, Round was made district superintendent of public schools for the county. He would be instrumental in helping establish a high school, an agricultural school, and was a supporter of the Manassas Industrial School for Colored Youth.

Above: The original cast iron hand-painted sign from H. D. Wenrich's Jewelry store at 9123 Center Street. Many people believed that the time, 3:43, marks the hour Abraham Lincoln died. In actuality, the hands are painted in this manner to present a balanced appearance.

Above left: Weir & Bro. Clearance Sale advertisement typical of the late nineteenth century. The store was located on the corner of Center and West streets from 1885 to 1917.

Members of the Breeden family, circa 1890. Left to right: Front row—Anna Ursula, Augusta Walser, Enos K., Blanche Regina; back row—Oliver E., Edwin A., Alfred C., Christian M., Enos S., and Robert H.

In 1869, the Brown School, named for Mary D. Brown of the Friends of Philadelphia, which supplied the funds, opened for African American children. Later, the Rosenwald Fund, which supported social issues, especially education for African Americans, provided dollars to help maintain the school, which finally located at the intersection of Liberty and Prince William streets. In 1884, another one-room schoolhouse, situated two and a half miles outside of Manassas in Lucasville, was constructed by parents for black children.

Right: George Carr Round as a young man in his Union army uniform. Born in Easton, Pennsylvania, Round enlisted in the Union Army while still in college. He was eventually assigned to the Army Signal Corps and is shown here holding his Signal Corps binoculars. His telescope holder sits on the table.

Below: An 1886 photo of the Hixson family and friends in front of their residence at 9319 Main Street. George Washington Hixson (1836–1925), standing on the porch with a hat on, served in the Prince William Rangers and in the Forty-third Battalion Virginia Cavalry (Mosby's Rangers). He served on the town council in 1875 and began the Manassas Cemetery shortly after the Civil War, later selling the land to the town for $1,000.

Left: Johnson family members and servants in front of their 1883 home at Clover Hill Farm. Purchased from Christian Mathis, the home was replaced after 1904.

Below left: Emma Chapman, personal servant/slave of Joseph Benjamin Johnson of Clover Hill Farm. After the Civil War, Chapman stayed on with the Johnson family until her death.

George Carr Round also helped write the 1873 town incorporation charter, which established a town council. A mayor, sergeant, clerk, and seven council members comprised the local government. Voters chose the first council, which served without compensation, and the council chose the mayor. Round was the first town clerk. The first mayor was Robert C. Weir, son of Liberia's William J. Weir. The first standing committees involved those needed by a growing community: streets, sidewalks, cemetery, fire department, assessments, and police regulations. The public water system began in 1874 with a well dug on East Center Street. Two buckets were purchased with which to draw water. By 1897, the town had six public wells.

Upon his 1877 marriage to Emily C. Bennett, George Carr Round became a fully transplanted citizen of Manassas. The Bennett family arrived in the area shortly before the First Battle of Manassas, and Emily, an only child, grew up in a home in the area near city park at the intersection of Sudley Road and Grant Avenue.

Right: Robert Carter Weir (1824–1905), son of William James and Harriet Bladen Weir of Liberia Plantation, served in the Confederate Army as a paymaster. He became the first mayor of the new town of Manassas in 1873 but resigned in 1874 because he moved out of the town of Manassas and opened a general store. In the 1890s, he donated land at 9235 West Street on which Trinity Episcopal Church stands today.

Below: "Harvesting on the Battle-field of Bull Run." An engraving of local farmers harvesting on the former battlefield lands. From *Harper's Weekly*, August 21, 1869.

HARVESTING ON THE BATTLE-FIELD OF BULL RUN.

Steam tractor and threshing machine at work in Brentsville around 1910. The J. I. Case steam tractor was an important piece of machinery on any farm. Farms that could not afford their own equipment hired tractor and threshing services. To operate the thresher (shown), a log cutter, or a plow, a belt was run from the small wheel above the rear wheel to the other machine. The rear wheel on this tractor is about 5' 6" high. Early steam tractors were powerful but slow and required a large quantity of water and fuel. It usually took at least three people to keep a steam tractor operating. By 1920, internal combustion engines replaced steam tractors for most farm work.

After their marriage, George and Emily Round moved into the Bennett homestead and reared three daughters and two sons.

The county, as required by the 1870 state constitution, organized a Board of Supervisors with six magistrates representing specific townships of Occoquan, Dumfries, Brentsville, Manassas, Gainesville, and Cole. In 1875, the state constitution was amended modifying the township system into magisterial districts, which continue to this day.

The Manassas Magisterial District, which also defined the school district, was bounded on the north by Piney Branch and Pageland Lane, on the east by Bull Run, on the south by Occoquan Run, and on the west by Broad Run.

In the first half of the twentieth century, homes and businesses were built close to the railroad tracks. The Geris family home stood south of the tracks at the corner of Main Street.

As Manassas grew, many Christian religious denominations came to build churches: Presbyterian (1867), Methodist Episcopal (1874), Episcopal (1874), Catholic (1878), Colored Baptist (1879), White Baptist (1884), and Grace Methodist (1892). Several of these denominations built their structures along Church Street, but the Manassas Church of the Brethren built theirs at Cannon Branch in 1895 while Bethel

Scandal rocked Manassas in 1872 when twenty-eight-year-old Confederate veteran and former commonwealth attorney James F. Clark was arrested and charged with abduction and carrying away sixteen-year-old Fannie Fewell to Baltimore and points west. A daughter of William Fewell, Fannie was staying with her married sister, Mrs. Benjamin Merchant, and met Clark at the home of Charles and Georgianna Hynson. Clark, a married man with several children, led Fannie to believe that he was divorcing his wife and wished to marry her. Giving credence to his story, Clark's family had left for King George County. Fannie seemed to be coquettish and undoubtedly welcomed his attentions. Various letters were passed between the two, and arrangements were made for Fannie to board a late-night train from Manassas to Washington.

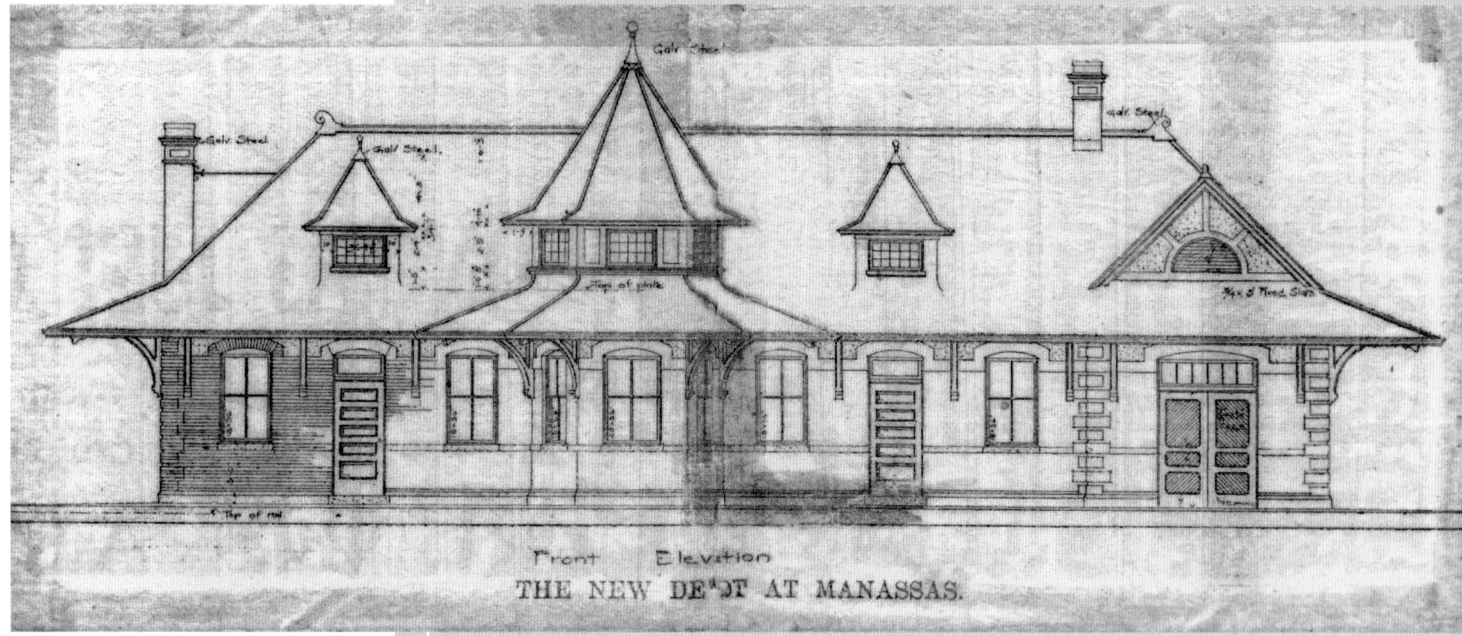

Artist's sketch of the Southern Railway Depot, 1914. The present depot is the third depot building on this site. An 1880s log frame depot built by the Richmond and Danville Railroad Company was replaced with a brick depot in 1904. A fire in 1914 burned this depot, and a new one, pictured here, was built on the 1904 foundation.

The pair traveled to various places, but Clark reneged on marriage and abandoned Fannie. Police helped her to reach her brother-in-law, who brought her back to Manassas. The family pressed charges against Clark. He was arrested by Sheriff Elias E. Conner and jailed at Brentsville. Fannie was under the care of Dr. Emlyn Marsteller for "nervous symptoms" and "hysterical spasms." Before a trial could be held, however, Fannie's brother Lucien, known as "Rhoda," Fewell resolved the matter himself. Armed with a pistol in each hand, he went to the unguarded jail next to Brentsville Courthouse, walked in, and repeatedly fired shots at Clark through the iron grating of his jail cell door. Witnesses reported seeing Fewell enter the jail and heard the shots. The sheriff came later with doctors to aid the prisoner and charged Fewell. Clark died within days, and Fewell was charged with his murder.

Clark's father, the prominent Reverend John Clark, engaged former governor and personal friend Henry A. Wise to assist in Fewell's prosecution. Reverend Clark, suspicious of the county that left his son unguarded, thought Wise, a charismatic speaker, could help Judge Charles E. Sinclair and the prosecuting attorney J. Y. Menifer. For the defense, Fannie Fewell's father hired two Civil War heroes, General Eppa Hunton, the hero of Ball's Bluff, and General William H. Payne. The defense introduced copies of correspondence to illustrate Clark's questionable intentions while the prosecution had Fannie Fewell testify her belief of Clark's promises.

By mid-November, oral arguments were complete and the jury sent out to determine a verdict. The jury returned after five minutes of deliberation, finding the defendant not guilty of the charges. The courthouse of spectators burst into loud applause showing they believed the brother had rightfully defended his sister's honor. Fewell's friends took him to Reid's Hotel across the street to celebrate and then back to Manassas.

Manassas Jail front view, circa 1925. The two men (James and Bob Jarman) were the town's jailors. The jail resembles a house more than a jail. (Courtesy of Ruth E. Lloyd Information Center, Prince William County Library)

After settling into Manassas as a lawyer and real estate entrepreneur after the Civil War, George Carr Round married a local woman, Emily Bennett. Together they raised five children, four of whom are pictured here. Their home was located on Bennett Drive off Grant Avenue.

Lieutenant George C. Round, a native of Wyoming Valley, Pennsylvania, was the son of Reverend William and Sarah Round. A third-year student at Wesleyan University in Middletown, Connecticut, when the Civil War broke out, he left to enlist in the First Connecticut Corps. Stationed at the present-day site of the North Carolina governor's mansion in Raleigh, Round was ordered by General William T. Sherman to climb to the top of the state capitol's dome and send a final signal noting the war's end. Without direct access to the top of the dome, Round scaled a lightening rod cable to reach the cast-iron crown. About halfway up, he crashed partway through the glass skylight above the rotunda's floor. Carefully, he extracted himself and climbed to the top. Lieutenant Round sent brightly colored signal rockets to Union forces encamped around Raleigh with the message "Peace on earth, good will to men," dedicating it to all the men who fought and died between 1861 and 1865. This signal marked the war's end.

Lutheran Church built theirs on Lee Avenue. A string of businesses along Main and Center streets opened. These included W. C. Wagener's Furniture; Weinrich's Jeweler; E. R. Conner and Company, selling meats and groceries; and Hynson and Wineburg's Hardware. Ira Cannon and Benjamin Cornwell were major building contractors. In 1869, the *Manassas Gazette* began publishing. By 1900, Brown and Hooff Lumber Company, Manassas National Bank, Prescott's Spoke Factory, and Bull Run Nurseries were in operation. Additionally, Mayfield and Yorkshire Brownstone Quarries, Taylor and Brown's Planing Mills, Donation Libeau's Brick Works, Cockrell's Nursery, and John Tillett's stone quarry were open. George Black operated a tannery across from George Trimmer's sawmill. Railroad Street ran next to the tracks on the north side where numerous African American families lived. The population was more than one thousand citizens.

Several important events launched Manassas into the twentieth century on a positive note. Southern Railway continued to expand. Northern investments advanced into Northern Virginia, further opening up the little village to the world beyond. After years of repeated attempts to move the county seat to Manassas, the railroad's influence finally brought the town success in 1892. Constructed of brownstone from local quarries, the fifth county courthouse was under construction for two years, built on land donated by Emily and George C. Round on the corner of Lee and Grant avenues. The Rounds liked the idea of this intersection being named for the two opposing Civil War heroes and insisted the intersection illustrated national reunification. Round oversaw the planting of silver maples on the courthouse lawn and down Grant Avenue. Both West Street and Grant Avenue advanced northward, becoming the next area of major construction.

Original All Saints Catholic Church built in 1879 at the corner of Center Street and Fairview Avenue. Today it houses the Reformed Presbyterian congregation.

C. A. S. HOPKINS, PRESIDENT C. M. HOPKINS, SECRETARY AND TREASURER

All claims for deductions must be made within five days after receipt of goods. We ship and take receipts "in good order" and the risk is yours after such receipts are signed. On special directions to ship goods by express, expressage must be paid by purchaser. To receive proper attention, all communications must be directed to the firm.

Manassas, Va., July 31, '09.

Mr. [illegible] Rice,

Manassas, Va.

Bought ...of **The Hopkins Co., Inc.**

Manufacturing Confectioners

All Goods F. O. B. Manassas.

Top: Bill head from the Hopkins Candy Factory, July 31, 1909. This is a transaction between the factory and Mr. W. M. Rice.

Above: Howard P. Young with his U.S. Mail wagon, circa 1900. Manassas was the central location for mail delivery. The mail came by train and was distributed by wagon.

When the courthouse and county seat moved from Brentsville in 1892, many families, such as those of Judges Sinclair and Thornton, also moved to Manassas. The clerk's and sheriff's offices and assessments were located on the first floor of the new court building. The court and County Board of Supervisors met on the second floor. Spittoons were liberally located near the defense and prosecution tables and elsewhere in the building. A small jury room easily conveyed shouting outside when juries became overly involved in their discussions. Court Day was more than a day when court was in session but was celebrated monthly by local people who came to town to sell livestock and farm supplies on the courthouse lawn.

Top: Rixlew Camp, 1904. In 1904, the U.S. Army held what have been called the first peacetime maneuvers. The Spanish-American War of 1898 had demonstrated that the army needed to improve its ability to equip, supply, and transport large numbers of troops in the field. The arena was the land upon which the Civil War battles of Manassas were fought. Close to twenty thousand soldiers camped on the lands from Bull Run to Thoroughfare Gap. More maneuvers took place in 1939.

Left: Brass souvenir medallion from the September 5–20, 1904, U.S. Army maneuvers in Manassas. Shaped like a canteen, the medallion has the Stone House on it.

Right: Hinge, from a shutter or light door, of the jail at Brentsville Courthouse. Made of cast iron and painted white, the hinge is two inches wide and about five inches tall. The courthouse and jail were built in 1820. In 1892, the county seat, and therefore the courthouse, moved to Manassas.

The Portner family, circa 1910. Anna and Robert Portner (1837–1906) are the adults in the front row. They met at a dinner party in Manassas at the home of Christian Mathis. The couple had thirteen children.

The year 1894 was important for Manassas and two individuals of diverse backgrounds: Robert Portner, a German immigrant, and Jennie Dean, a former slave and domestic servant. Both left their marks on Manassas and the townspeople. A refugee from potential Prussian military service, sixteen-year-old Portner arrived in New York in 1853 on a ticket paid for by an older brother. Learning English within a few years while working at odd jobs, he became a citizen and took his savings to Washington, D.C., at the outbreak of the Civil War. Once in the city teeming with the daily arrival of soldiers, he hitched a ride to nearby Alexandria and connected with another German.

Together they opened a grocery store supplying food and necessities for the armies. They expanded their booming business with the purchase of a small brewery. After the war, the partners split, and Portner kept the brewery. Within ten years, his success allowed him to buy a shipyard, start a construction company, set up a German-speaking bank, and dabble in real estate, eventually becoming a millionaire.

By contrast, Jane "Jennie" Serepta Dean was a native of Prince William County, freed from slavery by the outcome of the Civil War. Cheap land sales allowed her father, Charles, to buy his own farmland, but to maintain the mortgage payments, Jennie, the eldest child, had to go to work. With only a limited education, she went into Washington at fourteen to work as a domestic. She was affiliated with the Nineteenth Street Baptist Church, and

Advertising poster for Portner Brewing Company. Prior to creating his own bottled brew, Robert Portner shipped beer in kegs to hotels and inns and supplied his beer garden in Alexandria. Of the three brands of beer advertised here, the oldest is Vienna Cabinet, begun in 1873. The premium export lager Tivoli started production in 1894. Poster, circa 1895.

Above: Jennie Serepta Dean (1854–1913). Jennie Dean went to Washington to work as a domestic servant at the age of fourteen. Through her savings and solicitations of wealthy white philanthropists, she was able to open a private trade/academic school for African American youth in 1894.

its members soon connected her with many job opportunities. Over time, Dean performed a variety of tasks as live-in help for numerous families, saving as much money as she could from her meager wages. Her efforts not only helped pay off the family farm's mortgage but also helped her siblings pay for their education.

Visits to the Manassas area by both of these individuals influenced them to make major contributions to the town. Robert Portner came to a dinner party on the Manassas farm of Christian Mathis where he met his future wife, Anna. Upon Mathis's death, Portner bought much of his land and built a huge summer home, Annaburg, there for his family of thirteen children. Jennie Dean's frequent visits home to see her family led her to establish four Baptist missions for African Americans and spearhead the fundraising that established the Manassas Industrial School for Colored Youth. Portner had wealth to invest in a sumptuous summer home and parklands around his two-thousand-acre estate of Annaburg, and in a mammoth dairy at Liberia, and to build the luxury Prince William

Right: The Portner home "Annaburg" upon its completion in 1894. The residence, a combination of Colonial Revival with Neoclassical elements and Renaissance Revival, was either named for Castle Annaburg, Portner's former military academy in Prussia, or his wife Anna, or both.

Hotel. He also invested in a bank and operated two quarries. Dean relied on contributions from the wealthy, constant solicitations, volunteer help, and middle class white supporters to realize a down payment on a farm four miles west of the village and to build the foundation of a school for children of former slaves that would endure for fifty years. Both Annaburg and the Industrial School were completed in 1894, helping to open up opposite ends of town and encourage their future development.

By 1900, Manassas boasted several schools in addition to Ruffner and Brown elementaries. A donation from financier/steel magnate Andrew Carnegie allowed a library to be added to Ruffner School. The private Manassas Institute, founded by Misses Fannie and Eugenia Osbourn in the Baldwin House for white K–12 students taught a strict academic curriculum. At the public Ruffner School, some limited high school offerings were available until a separate Manassas High School was built. With the passage of a state law establishing public high school systems through state appropriations, Manassas established its own school district. Trustees approached the Osbourn sisters to make their institute public, which they did. In 1908, to meet the needs of the surrounding rural society, the Manassas Agricultural School opened,

Campus view, Manassas Industrial School. The large building on the left is Hackley Hall, the boys' dormitory (named for Mrs. C. B. Hackley), and the large one on the right is Howland Hall, the girls' dormitory. Howland Hall, named for the first large donor, Miss Emily Howland, was the first major building erected on campus. It was completed in time for the dedication ceremonies conducted by Frederick Douglass on September 3, 1894.

the first of its kind in Virginia. By then, overcrowding at Ruffner forced this school to be converted to an elementary school. In all of these endeavors, George C. Round was active.

In 1895, a telephone switchboard of the Manassas Telephone Company provided party line service to the town. Beginning in 1904, Esther J. Bell Randall served as the sole operator. The company was located over Bell's Store at Center and West streets. The *Manassas Journal* newspaper began publication in 1895, later absorbing the *Manassas Gazette.* The National Bank of Manassas and Peoples National Bank became important financial institutions. A

Above left: Swavely School (1924–1935) was a boys' preparatory school training for attendance at Annapolis Naval Academy or the army's West Point Academy. It was located on the present site of the Manassas Museum. The original walkway still leads to the site.

Above right: Ruffner School, Public School No. 1 in Manassas, was the first public elementary school built for white children in Virginia after the Civil War. It was the result of efforts by George C. Round and named for the first state superintendent, William Ruffner. It began as an elementary school and became a secondary school in 1907.

Left: The student body and teachers of Ruffner School in 1890.

downtown sawmill would be replaced by a lumber store. Sadly, the 1905 fire destroyed or damaged about thirty businesses and residences within the center of town, with an estimated loss of between $60,000 and $100,000. Most of the businesses were located on "Blossom Row," named for their builder, E. E. Blossom. People near the fire grabbed their buckets, filled them with water, and raced to help contain the fire. The path of winds limited the fire to a certain extent, and a hand-manned pump prevented the fire from crossing Center Street, but it was still a disaster. The cause of the fire was never determined. Town Council adopted a number of safety precautions, however, including building codes requiring the use of brick, stone, or

Top: The original Brown School, or "School No. 2," on Liberty Street was built for African American children in 1869. Financed by the Philadelphia-based Friends Society for the Aid and Education of the Freedman, the school was named for one of their group, a Mrs. Brown.

Above: A group of Brown School students and teachers circa 1890.

Fannie and Eugenia Osbourn were the daughters of Dr. and Mrs. Richard Keene Osbourn of Upper Marlboro, Maryland. Fannie, the eldest, came to Manassas in 1888 to attend Virginia's first Summer Normal or Teachers' Institute at the Methodist Church. She returned as a governess soon after. Within the year, Fannie started a private school in the residence of Isaac Baldwin located on the site of the present Manassas Museum. Once her sister Eugenia arrived in 1890, the sisters established a private school, the Manassas Institute, a college preparatory school. The Institute was located first on Center Street and then moved to Grant Avenue into a building constructed by Samuel Milnes on land donated by George C. Round, who became a trustee. The Osbourn sisters lived on West Street. By using the College Entrance Exam standards for their students, the school built an enviable reputation in the education field. In 1906, the standards of the institute became the basis of the county's first public high school curriculum.

Above: Eugenia Osbourn (1857–1951) in retirement. She followed her older sister Fannie to Manassas to build the Manassas Institute in 1896, a private college preparatory school.

Right: The Manassas Institute and later the Temple School of Music, where Eugenia and Fannie Osbourn first taught in Manassas, was located on Grant Avenue. It was originally the Manassas Institute and then became the Temple School of Music operated by Margaret Temple Hopkins, daughter of C. A. S. Hopkins, owner of the Hopkins Candy Factory. It is now a private residence: 9132 Grant Avenue. (Photograph by Don Flory)

Pupils and teachers at the Manassas Institute, the class of 1906–07.

Fannie had married a former student, F. Murray Metz. She became principal of the Manassas Institute while Eugenie taught several different subjects. After two years, the county built an addition to Ruffner School and the high school moved to that location on Lee Avenue. Later when Fannie passed away, Eugenia became the principal, serving until 1935.

The Temple School of Music, under the direction of Margaret Temple Hopkins, daughter of C. A. S. Hopkins, owner of the Hopkins Candy Factory, moved into the former Manassas Institute building. It eventually became a private kindergarten and elementary school until 1959. Today the building is a private home.

Southern Railway Engine 531 in Manassas in 1900. Built by Baldwin Locomotive Works in 1885, this 2-6-0 type locomotive is loaded with coal and ready to pull a freight train out of Manassas.

concrete for business construction. Fortunately, no businesses failed, but rather the destruction seemed to motivate townspeople to reinvest and reconstruct. Within ten years, a new modern U.S. Post Office, a second Prince William Hotel, Hibbs and Giddings Men's Clothing Store, the Hopkins Candy Factory, the Connor block housing the *Manassas Journal* newspaper, a theatre/opera house, and Conner's grocery-meat market were built. In 1907, the Hopkins brothers hired local architect Albert Speiden to design a modern factory building to house their growing candy business on Battle Street near the railroad track. C. A. S. Hopkins moved his family into a newly constructed house they called Tudor Hall built by Ira Cannon.

Conner's Opera House on Center Street was the first business to be electrified, using equipment Conner supplied himself in 1906 since the town had no services

Above: As viewed from the depot, the destruction caused by the Great Fire of 1905 is clear. The row of businesses fronting the railroad tracks burned down, giving a clear view of Center Street. The handwritten numbers on the photograph denote:

1. The entire block that was burned
2. 9108 Center Street (present-day Carmello's)
3. , 4. 9100 Center Street (present-day Manassas Clay)
5. 9405 Main Street (site of present-day Old Towne Inn)
6. 9407 Main Street (site of present-day Art Beat Gallery and Ashby Jewelers)

Left: Dr. and Mrs. J. Garland Hamner at their new home at 8902 Center Street about 1905. Dr. Hamner was minister of the Presbyterian Church 1899–1910. The house is a wood frame in a Colonial Revival style.

Carrie Nation came to Manassas at the turn of the century as the guest of Mrs. George W. Hixson on Main Street. A muscular, God-fearing woman often called the "Kansas Cyclone," Nation spoke widely and with passion for the Woman's Christian Temperance Union (WCTU). Her first husband died of alcoholism, and she became a vocal, one-woman crusader working for the prohibition of alcohol, always dressed in a black dress with a hat tied under her chin. Invited to Manassas at the request of builder Donation Libeau, she came with a Bible in one hand and a hatchet in the other, boldly entering saloons where she liberally smashed liquor bottles and a few windows. Whether Carrie Nation had any influence, in 1901 an Anti-Saloon League formed in Virginia, leading to the passage in 1903 of a stringent regulation for licensing saloons in places with fewer than five hundred residents. In 1908, Manassas was a "dry" town. A federal prohibition amendment to the U.S. Constitution was adopted in 1919 but repealed in 1933.

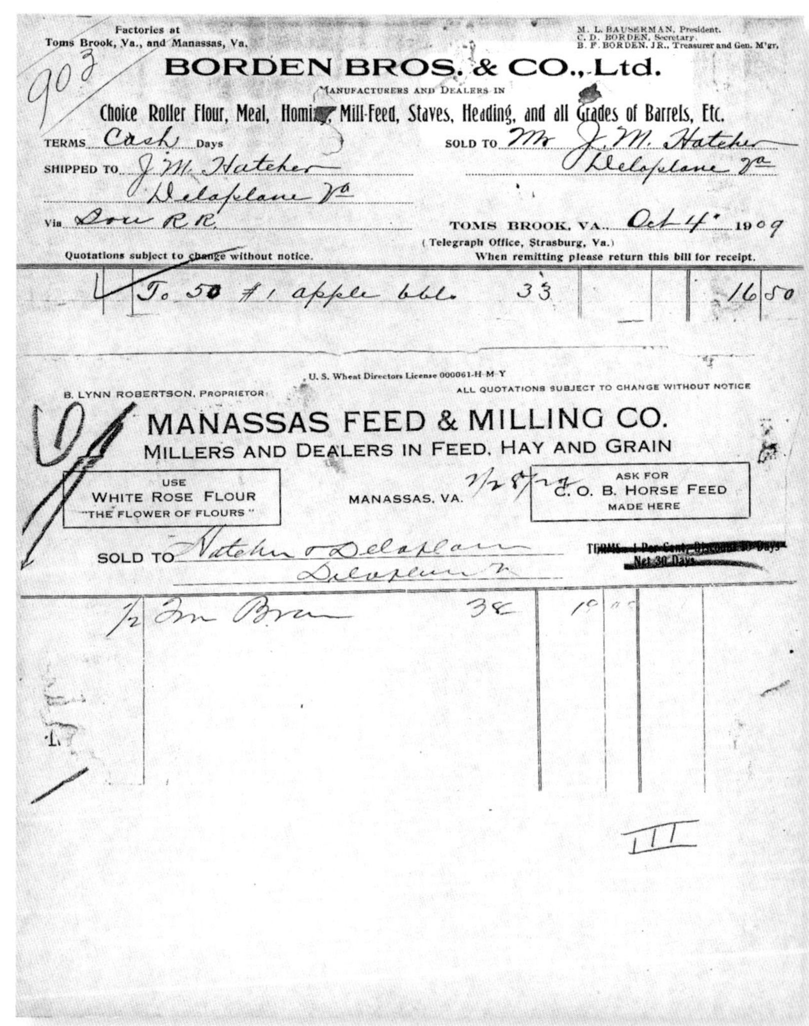

Factories at
Toms Brook, Va., and Manassas, Va.

M. L. BAUSERMAN, President.
C. D. BORDEN, Secretary.
B. F. BORDEN, JR., Treasurer and Gen. M'gr.

903

BORDEN BROS. & CO., Ltd.

MANUFACTURERS AND DEALERS IN

Choice Roller Flour, Meal, Hominy, Mill-Feed, Staves, Heading, and all Grades of Barrels, Etc.

TERMS Cash Days SOLD TO Mr J. M. Hatcher
Delaplane Va

SHIPPED TO J. M. Hatcher
Delaplane Va

Via Sou R.R. TOMS BROOK, VA. Oct 4 1909
(Telegraph Office, Strasburg, Va.)

Quotations subject to change without notice. When remitting please return this bill for receipt.

To 50 #1 apple bbl. 33 16 50

U. S. Wheat Directors License 000061-H-M-Y

B. LYNN ROBERTSON, PROPRIETOR

ALL QUOTATIONS SUBJECT TO CHANGE WITHOUT NOTICE

MANASSAS FEED & MILLING CO.

MILLERS AND DEALERS IN FEED, HAY AND GRAIN

USE
WHITE ROSE FLOUR
"THE FLOWER OF FLOURS"

MANASSAS, VA. 2/28/27

ASK FOR
C. O. B. HORSE FEED
MADE HERE

SOLD TO Hatcher & Delaplane
Delaplane

TERMS 1 Per Cent. Discount 10 Days
Net 30 Days

½ Ton Bran 38 19

Two bills of sale. Manassas Feed and Milling occupied the Hopkins Candy Factory after 1917. The bottom bill is dated 2/28/[19]27.

or power house. The first residence to be electrified was constructed about 1908 on a lot to the left of the original Town Hall on Center Street by builder Benjamin C. Cornwell for his family. In 1914, the original Town Hall, designed by Albert Speiden, was finished next door to Cornwell's house. It supplied space on the first floor for the Volunteer Fire Company, founded in 1892, and council chambers on the second floor. A power house was constructed on east Church Street, and the next year, water lines were laid down Center Street. Robert Portner personally paid to place gravel on Main Street up to the gates of his property. Dirt roads were still the standard, and street lamps were lit nightly by a lamplighter.

The first major event for the town was the Manassas National Jubilee of Peace staged on July 21, 1911, the fiftieth anniversary of the First Battle of Manassas. Ever the peacemaker, George C. Round was active with Union veterans and acquainted with many Confederate veterans. He conceived of the idea of a peaceful reunion of veterans from both sides to come together at Manassas and shake hands in peace on the battlefield. On Henry Hill the morning of July 21, 1911,

The original 1914 Town Hall at 9025 Center Street designed by architect Albert Speiden. The building was enlarged in 1930 with a two-story addition, and its original cupola was removed in the 1960s. After seventy-three years as the seat of municipal government, Town Hall was superseded in 1987 by a new four-story City Hall adjacent to the original building. Town Hall subsequently housed an exhibition center and offices for the Manassas Museum (1987–91) and the city's Visitor Center operated by Historic Manassas Inc. (1993–97). In 1997, the city's Voter Registration department moved into Town Hall, and the cupola was replaced in 2003.

This entrance at 9229 Portner Avenue is one of the four homes built by Donation Libeau for railroad workers. (Photograph by Bradley Edwards)

hundreds of Civil War veterans joined hands for peace. In the late afternoon, U.S. President William Howard Taft and Virginia Governor William Hodges Mann spoke to hundreds of spectators brought to town by the railroad for the ceremony on the courthouse lawn. Because of poor road conditions between Washington and Manassas plus the flooding of Willow Springs, President Taft almost missed the event. For the drive to Manassas from Washington, D.C., it took two replacement cars to get him out of road muck to arrive in the late afternoon, barely in time for his speech. Local girls representing every state in the union sang the Jubilee anthem "United," and Judge Thornton and Robert Portner opened their homes for receptions for dignitaries and veterans that night. Reconciliation was the hallmark of the day as old Confederate and Union soldiers put the past behind them to look forward toward the promise of the twentieth century. It would be another thirty years, however, before the Manassas battlefield would be declared a national historic landmark.

John Wiggin Prescott (1851–1913) was a developer and builder who constructed his home and numerous others along Prescott Avenue.

Governor William Hodges Mann and troops for the U.S. Cavalry and the Virginia State Militia marched with the old soldiers to the original battle site. At noon, the men lined up—blue and grey across from each other on Henry Hill. Then they marched toward each other where they clasped their hands in friendship solidifying national peace.

The fiftieth anniversary of the First Battle of Manassas was billed as a day of national reconciliation and called the Manassas National Jubilee of Peace. Heralded as an event for all people to enjoy, it was the idea of "Yankee" George C. Round, who was regarded as a sterling citizen even though he had been on the opposing side during the Civil War. Elaborate flags and bunting draped homes and businesses for the occasion. Heat from the sun was blistering, freely circulating the road's red dust. Crowds arrived early in the afternoon, vying for a seat around the grandstand on the courthouse lawn. For weeks, the Southern Railway promoted the event with posters of President Taft displayed in their many railroad stations and waiting rooms. Southern offered reduced round trip fares for everyone from all their stations.

Previous page, top: The Prince William County Courthouse at the corner of Grant and Lee avenues was built in 1892 on land donated by George and Emily Carr Round. On this lawn, President Howard Taft gave his address at the time of the National Jubilee of Peace in 1911. The anchors were donated years later by then Under Secretary of the Navy Franklin D. Roosevelt.

Previous page, bottom: Confederate veterans shake hands at the National Jubilee of Peace, July 21, 1911, on the Manassas Battlefield. (Library of Congress)

Above: George Carr Round, on the right, was the chairman of the 1911 National Jubilee of Peace. He stands next to the side of the banner denoting the Manassas Picket Post, Grand Army of the Republic (Union veterans). On the left is Lieutenant Colonel Edmund Berkeley representing the Ewell Camp, Confederate veterans.

Right: Southern Railway offered reduced round-trip fares to Manassas for the Peace Jubilee. A major event for Northern Virginia, President William Howard Taft and Governor William Hodges Mann headlined festivities on the courthouse lawn and the Manassas Battlefield.

MANASSAS
NATIONAL JUBILEE
Manassas, Va.
July 20-21, '11

A REUNION OF THE BLUE AND THE GRAY IN CELEBRATION OF THE 50th ANNIVERSARY OF THE FIRST BATTLE OF THE GREAT WAR FOUGHT AT BULL RUN, VA. (MANASSAS), JULY 21, 1861.

THE PRESIDENT OF THE UNITED STATES is expected to be at Manassas July 21, where he will be accorded a reception, later delivering an address, as will also the Governor of Virginia and other distinguished statesmen, who will be in attendance. Several Companies of Virginia State Militia and one or more Troops of the United States Cavalry will take part in the exercises.

At noon, July 21st, on Bull Run Battlefield, the veterans will be marshalled in review and the lines of the Blue and Gray will clasp hands in friendship on the scene of conflict fifty years ago. Other battlefields in that vicinity will be visited.

REDUCED ROUND-TRIP FARES
will apply from all stations on
Southern Railway

Dates of sale July 18-19-20 and for trains reaching Manassas by noon July 21st, including local train No. 10 of this latter date. Final return limit reaching original starting point not later than
MIDNIGHT JULY 24, 1911.

FOR FURTHER INFORMATION CONFER WITH LOCAL AGENT OR WRITE
L. S. BROWN, General Agent, H. L. BISHOP, Passenger Agent,
705 Fifteenth Street, N. W., Washington, D. C.

S. H. HARDWICK, Passenger Traffic Manager
H. F. CARY, General Passenger Agent

President William Howard Taft and Governor William Hodges Mann (standing, left of the president) in another view of the Jubilee festivities.

Seven-inch ribbon from the 1911 National Jubilee of Peace. The ribbon is white satin with gold thread.

Manassas citizens and businesses, including Mr. and Mrs. G. Raymond Ratclifffe whose home at 9136 Grant Avenue is shown here, decorated the town to welcome President Taft and hundreds of visitors.

Left: Albert Speiden (1886–1933), architect, in his Washington, D.C., office, possibly at 1403 New York Avenue NW, Washington, D.C. Speiden produced hundreds of designs for houses, movie theaters, churches, apartment buildings, and government buildings in the District of Columbia, Virginia, and California. Albert was proud that, at one time, he had done work for every church in Manassas.

Below: The Speiden Carper House at 9320 Battle Street. After Albert Speiden's 1901 marriage to Effie Lee Nelson, the newlyweds moved to Manassas in 1905 and into a house Speiden designed. They had two children: Thomas, who died in the 1918 influenza epidemic, and Virginia. Virginia Speiden Carper and her husband Lewis Carper made lasting contributions to Manassas, and many residents enjoyed their organ and piano music. Upon her death in 2006, Virginia bequeathed the house to the City of Manassas for a historic house museum.

Albert Speiden was an architect who, following the 1905 fire, was instrumental in the reconstruction of numerous brick buildings in Manassas that give the town its historic character. Most notable are the original Town Hall, the Hopkins Candy Factory, the U.S. Post Office, and the Masonic Building. He married Effie Lee, the daughter of Edwin Nelson, a deputy sheriff, long-time county clerk, and state legislator. Nelson donated the land for the Speiden home, which Albert designed, at 9320 Battle Street. Serving on the Town Council from 1909 to 1919, Speiden was instrumental in bringing modern

Left: Hopkins Candy Factory, 9406 Battle Street, from a 1910 postcard. When constructed in 1908, it was the largest building in the downtown. The Candy Factory operated from 1908 to 1917. Since then, it has been a milling and feed operation, a warehouse, and finally home for the Center for the Arts of Manassas/ Prince William County. The name "Candy Factory" has held on through the years. With approximately $2.5 million funded by the City of Manassas and the Commonwealth of Virginia Department of Transportation, the Candy Factory was renovated in 2001–2003.

utilities to the area. He also helped found the fire department, serving as its first president. Nearly every church or church renovation in Manassas exhibits his architectural designs. The Nelson family built a summer home and farm they called Robnel on land located today between Beauregard Avenue and Nelson Lane. Nelson Park, at the corner of Sudley Road and Grant Avenue is named for the C. P. Nelson family, who donated the land.

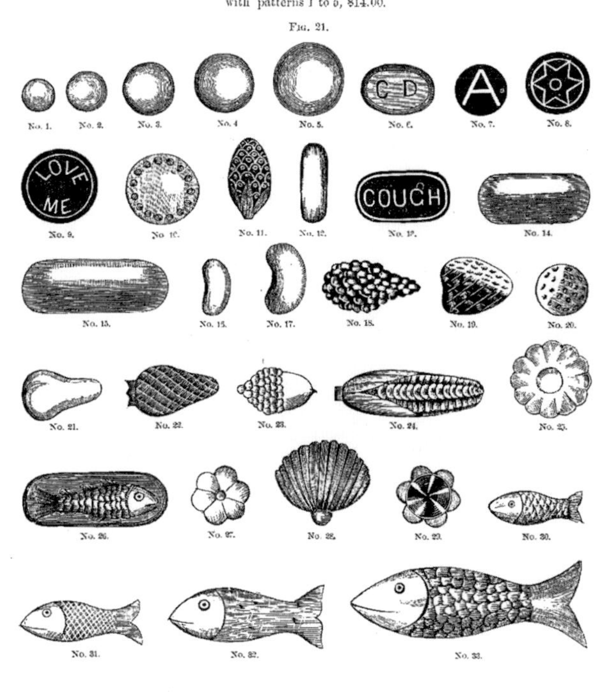

Right: Hard candies similar to ones made and sold by the Hopkins Candy Factory. This advertising sheet from Crandall and Godley shows candy purchasers how to order particular designs for their candies.

Previous page: Tudor Hall, an imposing home built on Tudor Lane by John A. Cannon for C. A. S. Hopkins, owner of the Candy Factory, in the late 1890s. Named after the little hamlet at the junction of the Orange & Alexandria and the Manassas Gap railroads, the residence was demolished in the 1960s. This demolition spurred a public outcry about lost history, which eventually led to the nomination of the Manassas National Register Historic District in 1988 and the designation as a Virginia Main Street community. In 2003, Manassas was one of five communities across the country to win a Great American Main Street Award presented by the National Trust for Historic Preservation.

Left: A 2008 view of the Confederate Memorial in the Manassas Confederate Cemetery. The eighty-three-foot-tall brownstone and marble monument is topped by a bronze Confederate soldier "at rest." The remains of 250 Confederate soldiers from the First and Second Battles of Manassas are interred here. Manassas is one of the few sites in the United States with several memorials for both the North and the South. (Photograph by Don Flory)

Old Town Manassas and surrounding area, February 2008. (Photograph by Roger Snyder, Ret. Director of Community Development, City of Manassas)

Chapter V

The Town Matures

1912–1952

Sunday in Manassas in the early part of the twentieth century generally meant attendance at one of the many churches in town, followed by a pleasant afternoon on the grounds of the Portner estate. The thirty-five-room air-conditioned Portner home was surrounded by beautiful trees, many imported, a large duck pond used for ice skating in the winter, and a swimming pool. Mr. Portner had even invented an early form of air-conditioning for the house. The thirteen Portner children freely mingled with town children and shared their toys, pony cart, and games. The estate ranged from Main Street to the Bull Run, encompassing the dairy farm at Liberia, an enclosed deer park with a hunting lodge where townsmen went hunting, and a farm specifically for show horses. A number of homes still standing on Main Street were built for the people who worked on the estate.

Mosby's Rangers' reunion flag made for the 1911 reunion in Manassas. The seventeenth annual reunion of Mosby's Rangers (Forty-third Virginia Battalion, Cavalry) took place in Manassas. The reunion dinner was co-sponsored by the United Daughters of the Confederacy, Manassas Chapter. The Stonewall Hotel, at the corner of Main and Center streets, hosted the dinner.

Town Council took several actions to modernize the town early in the twentieth century. Citizens had long desired public electric and water systems, but the council was reluctant to seek bonds or levy the taxes needed to pay for them. The 1905 fire served as a reminder that improvements were necessary. Finally, the council asked the Virginia General Assembly to amend the town charter to enable them to make contract loans and issue bonds with the approval of two-thirds of the council and

Above: Portner Gate House in 2008. Built by Robert Portner as a gatehouse for the entrance to his estate, Annaburg, this structure is an important landmark in Manassas. The architectural style mimics, in miniature, that of the Annaburg house. The stone for this and the Annaburg house came from Portner's quarry, the Portner Brownstone Company, at the end of Quarry Road in Manassas. Portner donated money to pave Main Street from Center Street to the gatehouse. (Photograph by Don Flory)

Above left: Main Street south of the railroad tracks, 1906. The sidewalks are being laid on the east side of Main Street looking north toward Center Street. Benjamin Clement Cornwell, the contractor, stands in front of the *Journal* newspaper office with laborer Dave Green to his right.

Left: Clarence Bryant on his roadster in 1914. Center Street is not yet paved, and horses and buggies share the road with the first automobiles in Manassas.

Laying water lines along Center Street in 1915. Before Center Street was paved, a water system was installed. At 9129 Center Street, the corner of Center and West streets, was the Hibbs and Giddings men's store (1888–1977); adjacent was H. D. Wenrich Jewelers at 9123 Center Street (1888–1960s). Across the street was William L. Smith groceries (1908–1917).

By 1916, Center Street had been paved. At the corner of Center and Main streets, the Peoples Bank Building held a variety of offices, including a post office, attorneys, real estate, a dentist, a barber, and a cobbler. Across the street, C. E. Nash's hardware store, at 9071 Center Street, sold farm implements, seed, and general hardware.

Center Street, Manassas, Va.

a majority of the voters. The first bond requests failed miserably until residents saw firsthand the damage fire could do. With the courthouse debt paid, seventy-five residents petitioned the council to use bonds up to $50,000 to improve the water system, provide electricity, and improve streets. Sadly, low interest rates drove serious bids away until 1913 when a $75,000 bond was finally approved.

Once public utilities were agreed upon, and the bonds issued, the town created two new positions: a treasurer to manage money and a superintendent of public works to manage utilities. James E. Nelson became the first treasurer while George L. Rosenberger became the first superintendent. In 1915, town council, officers,

Above: Grant Avenue continued to develop with homes such as "Edgemore," a large two-story frame stuccoed house with a large one-story columned porch at 9112 Grant. It was built around the turn of the nineteenth century for Dr. R. E. Wine and purchased by Dr. L. S. Houf, father of Mrs. Thomas E. (Marjorie) Didlake. Mr. and Mrs. Didlake endowed the Didlake School in 1965. Today's Didlake Inc. bears his name.

Left: Fourth of July Parade, circa 1920, on Grant Avenue.

This is the second Southern Railway Depot on the original location. Destroyed by fire in 1912, it was rebuilt in 1914 and restored in 1997 by the City of Manassas. The Prince William Hotel is in the right background.

and the fire department moved into the new town hall. Cost for the building plus heating and plumbing was $5,672. Public utilities would continue to concern the council for many years to come as tax assessments for more than one thousand citizens never kept pace with the treasury's rising deficit.

The third railroad station, built by Southern Railway in 1914, was expanded by thirty-two feet beyond the previous building and is a local landmark still in use. Placating segregation, there were two waiting rooms, one for African Americans and one for whites, each on either side of the ticket master's office. In the tower, two small windows allowed views of the tracks from inside of the building. In 1993, Norfolk Southern Railroad donated the depot to the city. The city bought the land on which the station stands, enabling the city to restore the building to its 1914 glory for commuter rail service.

Other individuals have contributed their skills and money to creating the historic character that is Manassas today. In his will, circa 1900, Robert Portner provided for a new brick Masonic Lodge building on Center Street. Benjamin C. Cornwell, who owned a construction company, constructed numerous other buildings in town, such as the Grace Methodist Church and several brownstone homes. Cornwell often worked from designs provided by Albert Speiden, and he obtained the first contract to build concrete sidewalks in town. On Portner Avenue, Donation Libeau, an immigrant teetotaler from New Zealand, built four houses for railroad employees. Meanwhile, on the corner of West Street and Lee Avenue, John Dennis Baker expanded his father's funeral business to encompass a fourth of the block. In 1928, he established the first ambulance service, operating it into the 1950s.

Above: Virginia Speiden Carper with her dollhouse, circa 1916. Made in 1914 for Virginia by her father Albert Speiden, the dollhouse was lovingly cared for by the family for more than ninety years. The number of furnishings grew over time until the house and yard filled to resemble our own full houses. Visitors to 9230 Battle Street recall the house set in the living room and decorated for the holidays.

Left: The town's first jeweler, H. D. Wenrich, standing in front of his original store around 1900, arrived in Manassas in 1887. The family lived in the rear of the store. In 1905, Wenrich built a new stone structure next to this building at 9125–9127 Center Street and had this house moved to Grant Avenue. By 1911, the Wenrich family built a new house at 9026 Grant Avenue. Wenrich also pursued photography and took a number of pictures, which he made into postcards and sold in his store.

The Manassas Industrial School—Engage the Heart and the Hand

Years of fundraising from philanthropists in Boston, New York, Baltimore, and Washington enabled Jennie Dean to realize her dream and purchase one hundred acres of farmland near the railroad tracks west of town. Local funds supplemented Northern philanthropy. Designed as a private residential institution for African American youth, the school provided both academic and vocational training. Jennie Dean campaigned not only to improve education for the children of former slaves, but also to keep families whole and self-sustaining.

Howland Hall, named for Emily Howland who donated the funds, was the first building constructed, completed in time for the 1894 dedication, which featured Frederick Douglass as speaker. Susan B. Anthony donated $12,000 to the school, and Andrew Carnegie built the library. By the turn of the century, more than 150 students were enrolled for an academic year lasting from October through May. Operating expenses were offset by maintaining an active farm and varied industries from which students learned agriculture, carpentry, shoemaking, sewing, domestic arts, and animal husbandry. Academic instruction included mathematics, natural sciences, geography, physiology, music, literature, history, and English. Students came from all over Northern Virginia and boarded at the school and paid their expenses partly through their work on campus. Always financially hard pressed, the school survived as a private institution until 1937. At that time, a joint board of control made up of Prince William, Fairfax, and Fauquier counties purchased the entire school complex and established a regional high school for African Americans. This arrangement lasted into the 1950s when Fairfax and Fauquier opened their own schools of a similar nature. In 1954, Prince William consolidated students from Brown School into a regional high and elementary school on the property. A new building was constructed in 1959 and named to honor Jennie Dean. Upon integration in 1966, it continued as a high school. In 1977, when the City of Manassas took over the building, it became a middle school. In 1991, it became Jennie Dean Elementary School.

In 1914, Grace E. Metz was a first-year teacher at a one-room schoolhouse, formerly a private school operated by Mary Dogan. The Dogans of Groveton rented a room in their home to Metz when she was hired as the first public school teacher for the "Battlefield School" as it was called, referring to its location. The students ranged from grades one through high school. A recent graduate of a Normal Teachers School, Metz considered herself a "greenhorn," but she soon adjusted to teaching around a central pot-bellied stove, instructing all grade levels. Her initial salary was $45 a month. In her second year, the county opened a bigger two-room school and paid her $90 a month. After three years, she left Groveton to teach at Bennett Elementary School in Manassas. Today, Metz Middle School is named for her.

Above left:: Grace Metz, standing far right, in 1923 with her elementary and secondary students at Bennett School. Her initial salary was $45 a month.

Above: Grace Metz teaches a science class in 1953.

Left: The 1950 graduating class of Osbourn High School at Bennett School.

James M. Keys Jr. of Manassas was a member of the World War I Wildcat Division, Eighty-first Infantry Division. Originally named the "Stonewall Division" in honor of General Thomas J. "Stonewall" Jackson, they sailed for Europe on July 31, 1918, and participated in major engagements in Meuse-Argonne and Alsace-Lorraine, France. This may be the same person who opened a new grocery and filling station in 1939, 1.5 miles south of Manassas on Route 234.

J. Hendley Johnson of Clover Hill Farm at the time of his enlistment. He was one of the Johnson brothers who fought in World War I. He was a member of the American Expeditionary Forces, the United States Armed Forces sent to Europe in World War I.

World War I seemed far away for town residents until young men like the three Johnson brothers, Hendley, Wheatly, and Benjamin, of Clover Hill were drafted. The U.S. government requisitioned trains to transport troops from throughout the country to camps in Virginia and then overseas. If a train stopped in Manassas, townspeople would meet it with food and drink. The Johnson brothers survived their wartime experiences, but not so fortunate was Sergeant G. Oliver Lynch, who served in the American Expeditionary Forces. In June 1921, his remains were returned to Manassas from France. The flag-draped casket was immediately taken to the little wood All Saints Catholic Church on the corner of Center and Fairview streets for a funeral celebration. A large assemblage of friends and relatives of many faiths flocked to the service and reverently escorted the body to its final resting place in the town cemetery on Center Street for his re-interment. An army honor guard escorted the body from the church to the graveyard with full military honors. In memory of all of the county's fallen soldiers of World War I, local citizens planted commemorative trees along Lee Avenue on Armistice Day in 1925. This helped beautify the neighborhood and commemorate the fallen.

The 1936 sophomore class of Manassas High School. Their teacher, Emily Johnson, is seated in the front row, seventh from the left.

Even in the early 1900s, public schools were not always "free." Overcrowding at Ruffner School forced the intended agricultural school building to become Bennett Elementary School, named for the previous landowner Maitland C. Bennett. Tax dollars were inadequate to support the school, and the running deficit forced parents to pay tuition the last month in 1920 to keep the school open. The Alumni Association of Manassas High School paid to get a gymnasium built on Peabody Street, and they maintained it until 1936. The efforts of alumni, civic groups, and patrons in 1926 helped pass a $50,000 bond for a new high school for white students. A County School Board, established in 1925, had a superintendent's office in two rooms of the courthouse.

A group of local children in the 1920s were, left to right, Francis L. Cannon, Mattie Hooe Cannon Parrish, Anna Lee Hooe, and Mary Aileen Cannon Adams. (Courtesy of Mattie Cannon Parrish)

In the 1930s, the school superintendent, who also served as business manager and executive, was Richard Challice Hayden. The School Board oversaw the textbook business and employed an office clerk. Superintendents had four-year appointments and were paid partially by the State Board of Education, partially by the County Board of Supervisors, and partially by the School Board. He oversaw the white schools and conferred with the African American elementary schools, which were overseen and funded by the Jeanes Fund, created by a wealthy Philadelphia Quaker to support rural schools in the South. Unlike the free public schools for white students, African American students and their families paid tuition to the Manassas Industrial High School. Evelyn Fields remembered her parents paying about $3 a month to send her there, enabling her to become a teacher. Average teacher salaries in the 1930s were about $2,000 higher in white schools than in African American schools.

From 1909 until 1935, Manassas was home for Eastern College, followed by Swavely Prep School, both located on the Baldwin property, the site of the museum today. A checkered existence led to the demise of both schools while the Great Depression supplied the final blow.

Agricultural High School in Manassas, 1935. The quiz on the blackboard reads:

1. (a) Define forestry, a true woodland, & farmland and a timber tract
   (b) Give the distinctions between forestry & agriculture
2. (a) Give the features of the most general or recent classifications of farms
   (b) Give the best classifications of forest regions in the U.S.
3. (a) Give the functions of roots; types of roots & 3 examples of each
   (b) Describe the absorption of food by roots—through what 2 ways . . .

A collage of images of Eastern College Conservatory for Girls and Young Women (1921–1922), which offered a high school and junior college curriculum. Between 1909 and 1920, it had been a school for boys named Eastern College. Located on the grounds of the Manassas Museum. (Courtesy of William Hill Brown)

In 1927, with government growing in complexity, voters changed the local government structure to include a town manager. Managing a growing government became too involved for part-time councilmen. The first town manager was William R. Smith, hired in 1927. He was soon replaced by William F. Cocke, who served until his death in 1941. The five elected Town Council members continued to elect one of their number as mayor. In 1921, Harry P. Davis was chosen mayor, and he served until 1963 when Harry J. Parrish succeeded him. The builder Benjamin Cornwell served as a council member in the 1920s.

George Trimmer built an eight-by-ten-foot "lock-up" or jail for the town on Quarry Road for $104.75. In 1930, 124 street lights shone on the streets and cost $105 per light per month. The well-organized volunteer fire department quickly responded to the siren echoing throughout the town from on top of the town hall. An annual carnival begun in 1924 provided funding for the fire department and fun for the townspeople. When four young men were killed by a train crossing Grant Avenue in 1922, the need for the town to supply night watchmen for the major train crossings came under tremendous scrutiny. Not able to afford to cover five crossings, the Council agreed to put watchmen on duty for sixteen hours a day at Main and Fairview avenues. Grant Avenue and West and Battle streets were each assigned a watchman for twelve hours daily. Automatic signals and warnings replaced the watchmen in 1945.

In the late 1920s, several decisions impacted the way Manassas conducted its business. The town joined the Virginia League of Municipalities to improve local government, with Mayor Davis serving as the first small town president in 1933. Rural electric lines were sold off, and major streets such as Route 28/Centreville Road were hard surfaced. By now, J. W. Prescott had extended the street named for him to connect with Centreville Road, and a number of homes were being built there and along Maple and Cherry streets. As the Great Depression of the 1930s began to erode the national economy, the little town of Manassas could not escape the fall-out. A serious drought hit the area in 1930 and 1931 causing considerable suffering countywide. Fortunately, heavy rains in early 1931 helped the Red Cross normalize conditions.

The town was able to survive the Depression owing to the help of numerous federally sponsored programs. A large new post office on Church Street was built with federal funds while several construction projects on Grant between Lee and Center streets were completed with funds from the Federal Reconstruction Corporation. The Civil Works Administration funded sewer and street construction on Portner Avenue and Battle Street. The Federal Emergency Relief Administration maintained a regional office in Manassas once it supplanted the Works Progress Administration. Businessmen such as E. R. Conner and Joseph L. Bushong posted National Recovery Administration (NRA) Blue Eagle signs in their windows to indicate their early support for the New Deal program. Though membership in the NRA was voluntary, businesses that did not display the eagle were very often boycotted. Virginia Gas Distribution Corporation hired many men to lay gas lines. The Rural Electric Cooperative Administration helped organize the Prince William Electric Cooperative through a loan. A municipal airport opened just west of town in 1932, on the site of the Manaport Shopping Center. At Lake Jackson, developer Charles Alpaugh hired workers starting at twenty cents an hour to build the Lake Jackson Dam, which continues to function. A two-year project, the dam was eventually sold to Virginia Public Service, the forerunner of Virginia Electric and Power.

In 1914, the state General Assembly enacted laws providing for agricultural extension work in cooperation with the U.S. Department of Agriculture. With federal funds appropriating initial efforts via the Smith-Lever Act and state support, the Prince William County Board of Supervisors could authorize funds to pay for county extension agents. These agents helped save Virginia farmers during the Depression. Manassas had one agent in the early 1930s, Frank D. Cox, who was later assisted by Alice Webb. Farmers and their wives could come to them for advice and assistance. Some of the farmers, unable to afford gasoline, stripped down their cars and hitched them up to a team of horses to come into town.

In 1930, the Manassas Town Council proposed that a landing strip be constructed along Route 234 north of Manassas. At that time, the population of Manassas was 1,215 and the mayor was Harry P. Davis, for whom the airport is named. In 1964, the airport moved to its current location and became the Manassas Regional Airport. Today's Manaport Shopping Center is named for the airport.

James H. Payne (1916–2007) is seated in an airplane at the original Manassas Airport. He served for thirty-four years on the town and city councils and as vice mayor, in addition to serving on the Manassas Airport Commission for several years.

Above: Building the Lake Jackson Dam on Bland's Ford, 1927. Construction began in 1927 and took several years to complete. During the Civil War, pickets from Company A, Eighth Louisiana "Creole Guards" were stationed there. After the war and into the early twentieth century, the Occoquan River only powered two small sawmills. Charles W. Alpaugh (1876–1957) changed all that. He built and sold his three-hundred-foot-long dam that rose twenty-five feet from the base to Virginia Public Service, the forerunner of Virginia Electric and Power, and concentrated on developing the surrounding lands for city vacationers. The first lot sold for $79.

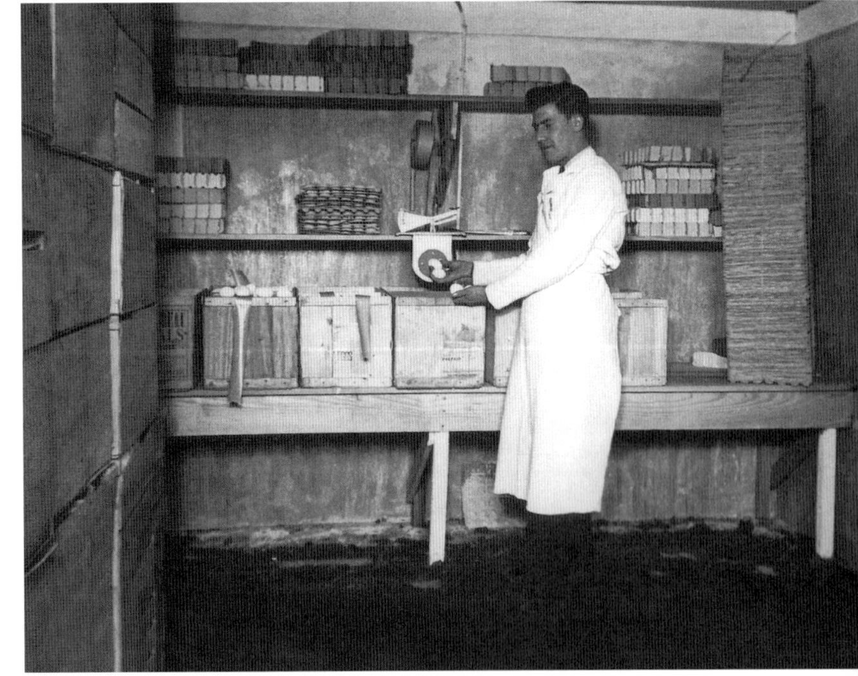

Right: Manual egg testing, 1936. Many patent applications for automatic egg testing devices were filed in the 1930s, but Walter Scudd of Manassas judged the freshness, approximate age, and recommended use for a chicken egg by hand.

They called these conveyances "Hoover Carts." Cox claimed local farmers referred to themselves as well-fed characters wearing patches on top of patches. Both agents married locally.

In this era, neighbors helped each other through churches, schools, or social groups. The Girls Tomato Clubs and Boys Corn Clubs for teens thrived while women formed an auxiliary affiliated with the State Home Demonstration agents. These groups had been active for nearly twenty years before the Depression hit. In many town yards, family gardens sprouted up next to spring flowers. In 1933, ten ladies chartered the new Manassas Garden Club, one of the original groups founded by the Virginia Federation of Garden Clubs. The first leader was Norma Young Cooksey. Other members included Marjorie Hough Didlake, Bettie Holden Hutchinson, Ruth Round Hooff, Bessie Virginia Benson Lewis, and Lelia Green Dowell.

Top: These four stone walls and silo are all that remain today of the 1923 Barrett barn next to Sunnybrook Golf on Sudley Road north of Manassas. The stones used to build the barn were originally gathered by slaves for the Dogan farm (now the Bull Run Shopping Plaza) prior to the Civil War.

Right: Democratic Party Rally in Manassas, 1938. After the United States entered World War I, President Woodrow Wilson appointed Herbert Hoover (1929–1933) head of the Food Administration. Hoover cut consumption of foods needed overseas and avoided rationing at home. The verb "Hooverized," which means making do with less, emerged at that time. Here, a car without an engine has a sign on it that says "I voted for Hoover in 1928, look at me now."

Left: "Confederate Ram Manassas Attacking the U.S.S. Brooklyn": 1920s color advertising card. W. F. McLaughlin & Company decorated its coffee tins with historical incidents and themes. The illustration was on the coffee tin, and the card was included with the coffee.

Below: Manassas Garden Club, 1958. Founded in 1933, the club has done a great deal to beautify the city with its flower, garden, and tree plantings and other civic endeavors.

Both men's and women's service groups kept busy during these years. Organized in 1913 at Clover Hill, the Bethlehem Good Housekeeping Club, a name suggested by Emily Johnson and derived from the defunct Bethlehem Baptist Church once located near Clover Hill, celebrated its twenty-fifth anniversary in 1935. In 1941, they published the first early county history, funded by the Works Progress Administration Federal Writers Project and titled *Prince William, The Story of Its People and Places.* The Junior Woman's Club, begun by thirteen women in 1931 under the auspices of the Woman's Club, only accepted young unmarried women. Annual dues were one dollar.

One woman, Gladys Dinges Bushong, initiated several organizations. She organized an Eastern Star Chapter to the men's Masonic Order, served as the local executive director of the Tuberculosis Association, and was active in the Woman's Club and the women's auxiliary at Trinity Episcopal Church. Bushong wrote a weekly column called "People, Places and Things" for the *Journal Messenger* and was an active proponent for local history until her death at ninety in 1974. In 1949, her daughter, Frances Bushong Saunders, was the first woman elected to serve on Town Council.

Men's civic clubs had a longer history than women's groups and were involved in the town's many projects. The Volunteer Fire Company was composed of nearly all the able-bodied men in town. A women's auxiliary helped raise money for equipment and uniforms. The Bull Run Hunt, began in 1911, was reactivated in 1939 by William Wheeler, Charlie Lynn, Carl Kincheloe, Raymond Jackson Ratcliffe, Conway Seefey, Charles Walton "Nubbins" Lewis, and others. They rode with hounds up and down the farmlands along Sudley Road (or "Whiskey Road" as they called it) and Centreville Road to the battlefield, hunting foxes. Hunt breakfasts were often held at the McBrydes' home "Winterset" where Godwin Drive now cuts through from Sudley Road or at "Paradise," the home of C. C. Lyon located behind the pond at

Manassas Town Council in the early 1950s included, left to right, Ferris Gue, William Hill Brown, Frances B. Saunders (the first woman elected to the council), G. Wallace Hook, Mayor Harry P. Davis, Hunton Tiffany, Town Manager Jim Ritter, and Roy Doggett. In 1946, the town budget was $21,852, of which $8,700 was allocated for streets and the balance to operations, including police, garbage collection, fire department, and street cleaning/snow removal.

Prince William Democratic Committee meeting at the Old Courthouse in October 1948. Virginia was known as a Democratic state well into the 1970s.

Bull Run Shopping Center. Once farmers began selling their farms, the hunt moved to the Catharpin-Haymarket and Nokesville areas, leaving the county. Until well into the 1960s, there were seventeen farms along Sudley Road between Manassas and the battlefield. Only the small airport located on ninety-five acres where Manaport Shopping Center is today broke the farming landscape. Remnants of Sunnybrook Farm run by John Barrett and his four sons remain nearby today in the form of the old stone barn walls near the Sunnybrook Golf driving range. The stones used for the barn were originally gathered by slaves prior to the battles and used for fences on properties located in that area.

Above: Lap desk owned by Sydnor Ferguson. Sydnor Ferguson (1846–1904) had just turned seventeen when he joined Mosby's Rangers in November 1863. After the Civil War, he attended college and seminary and was ordained a minister in the Methodist Church. Reverend Ferguson was a circuit preacher who traveled from Leesburg to Manassas and Front Royal. He used this desk in his travels, first by horse and buggy and later by train.

Right: "Doodlebug," a vehicle made from a tractor. F. R. Hynson and J. E. Bradford, partners in the Hynson & Bradford Radio Store, pose with this 1939 "hybrid" vehicle.

Late 1930s automobiles parked on Lee Avenue in front of recently demolished apartment buildings next to the Old Courthouse. The white columns of Bennett School are in the distance.

Deaconess Board of the First Baptist Church, 1952, in the church sanctuary. Women's church groups raised money for charity and helped prepare for services and communions.

Nearly all of the area farms were dairy farms with cattle, pigs, and horses completing the setting. Milk was usually shipped by truck, driven by local drivers to Thompson's Dairy in Washington, D.C. Edgar Renn Conner's farm had numerous outbuildings and a barn behind the house where he slaughtered cattle for his store on Center Street. He kept tenants on a cattle farm called Blooms in the area of the present-day Blooms Crossing subdivision of Manassas

Edgar Conner on his farm (Blooms) in Manassas Park, winter 1935–1936. Conner is seated holding the dog in an oxcart.

Lebanon Hall in the 1890s. This large, two-story frame house has a high gable in the front. According to one source, there was an earlier farmhouse or tenant house on the site that was part of the Liberia tract. The name "Lebanon Hall" is said to have come from the cedar allegedly used in construction, but a 1979 occupant said it was made of Georgia pine. The owner, E. R. Conner, owned a meat market and grocery store in Manassas and a 460-acre farm in the Manassas Park area. Conner was a longtime member of the Manassas Town Council and a delegate to the Virginia Assembly from 1940 to 1944.

Lebanon Hall as it appears today at 9014 Sudley Road. (Photograph by Don Flory)

Park. Blooms was used by General Johnston as his headquarters during the First Battle of Manassas. In town, Conner constructed a lovely Victorian home with his mother on Sudley Road, which they named "Lebanon Hall." Similarly, the Johnson brothers, now the fourth generation at Clover Hill, supplied fresh meat and produce for the local food stores.

Farmers came into town on Saturdays to purchase supplies. While wives shopped, the men found their way to Cornwell's gasoline station to sit around his potbelly stove and chat. Ladies had a restroom nearby with rocking chairs, where they could rest, freshen up, and compare purchases. Hibbs & Giddings and Hynson Department Store sold men's suits for $10 and shoes for $3 to $5. For some, however, even these prices were unaffordable.

Cornwell's Garage in 1947, a service station and grocery store selling American Gas.

Farmers bought only necessities like salt, pepper, and coffee. Orrin Kline Sr.'s mother baked her own bread, cakes, and pies. She canned vegetables for their growing family. She used a scrubbing board in a washtub to clean clothes. Chickens were the usual Sunday dinner. Hogs supplied pork and bacon. Homemade ice cream, a summer treat, was made with ice stored during the winter. Wood-burning stoves kept the Klines warm in cold weather.

Joseph Bushong in his third store, 1932. J. J. Bushong bought Charles E. Fisher and Son Grocery in 1915 and operated it in different locations in the downtown until 1942. A 1923 ad said "delivers the goods at your door, clean groceries at the right prices. Do not rob your body of good fresh vegetables & fruits."

To publicize the growing dairy industry in Northern Virginia, the Piedmont Dairy Festival Association of eleven counties and the cities of Alexandria, Fredericksburg, and Washington, D.C., was formed. The annual festival was held on the grounds of the Portner estate for six years in the 1930s until Manassas finances could no longer support it. Thousands of people came into town for the festivities. The streets were festooned with flags and bunting, and a parade with floats, marching bands, and young girls dressed as milk maidens went through town on Center Street. Young ladies, chosen from surrounding counties, formed a "court," with one of them crowned queen of the festival. Politicians made speeches. Lois Cornwell

Edgar Renn Conner was a prominent Manassas citizen. He and wife Anna Ursula Newman raised three daughters, Elevere Conner Cox, Anna Virginia Conner Ratcliffe, and Walser Conner Rohr, and one son, Edgar R. Conner Jr. Conner farmed two sites—Lebanon Hall and Blooms Farm—and dealt in real estate and building. He constructed several buildings along Center Street in 1907 after the 1905 fire, including Conner's Meat Market and Conner's Opera House for a variety of entertainments, recitals, and meetings. He was a director of the People's National Bank, served in the House of Delegates representing Prince William and Stafford counties in the 1940s, and was on the County Democratic Party Committee. He also was a member of the Town Council for a number of years.

Conner was instrumental in completing the Manassas Battlefield Museum and acquiring the Stone House for the National Park Service to operate after 1941. He received many awards from the Virginia Agricultural Extension Service and served as a charter member of the Maryland-Virginia Milk Producers Association. Through his efforts, trains made daily stops at Blooms Farm to pick up milk for delivery into Washington.

In the 1940s, young ladies of the Manassas Junior Women's Club, dressed as the "Gay Nineties" singing group, entertained the District Woman's Club. Pictured are, left to right standing, Walser Conner Rohr, Virginia Conner Ratcliffe, Elizabeth Lynn, and Dot Bryd; seated, Kitty Arrington, Frances Saunders, and Gilley Kincheloe.

Moore vividly remembered her mother operating a food stand on their front lawn next to the town hall. Mrs. Cornwell sold hot dogs, lemonade, homemade pies, cakes, cookies, and coffee to spectators.

Life in the 1930s was simpler, and people made do with what they had. Children freely walked to friends' homes and played together on swings and in sandboxes; they enjoyed outdoor games and snacks that brought them and the neighborhood together in a spirit

Top: The June 23, 1933, *Fairfax Herald* began an article "Dairying Festival":

Northern Virginia dairy interests plan a festival this fall that will, on a small scale, be like the annual apple blossom festival of the Valley, and last week, in Manassas, the Piedmont Dairy Festival Association was organized with Richard S. Hynson, Manassas, president; John M. Kline, vice president for Prince William; Frank D. Cox, county agent for Prince William, secretary; etc. The association is composed of dairymen of Fairfax, Fauquier, Prince William, Loudoun, Orange, Stafford, Culpeper, Madison, Stafford and Spotsylvania Counties. It is planned to have the festival October 31. A queen of the festival with ladies in waiting are to be selected, and the queen will preside over a mammoth parade with floats and other features in which the dairy herd improvement associations, the 4-H Clubs, school children, and possibly military organizations, and numbers of bands will be part. The festival will close with a ball at night. It is stated that the dairy interests in Fairfax County are taking much interest in the proposed festival, which is to be a yearly event. Here is a group of milkmaids from 1933.

Bottom: Storefront display for the Piedmont Dairy Festival. The festival highlighted the importance of milk production for Manassas in the 1930s.

of camaraderie. If children misbehaved, the community telephone party line soon relayed it to their parents.

On Memorial Day, the Manassas Chapter of the United Daughters of the Confederacy and their children marched to the Confederate Cemetery to lay fresh flowers at the base of the monument. Lois Cornwell Moore was reminded that her great-grandmother, Emma Williams Davis, dyed the fabric of her wedding dress red with beet juice to make it into the Prince William Cavalry flag that her husband carried in the First Battle of Manassas.

In 1934, an eighteen-year-old named Edgar Rohr came to town to

At the Piedmont Dairy Festival, October 11, 1935, held on the grounds of the Portner estate, Annaburg, the queen, Miss Mary Elizabeth Nelson, and her court assemble before the ball. Young women representing all of the participating counties competed for the crown.

Center Street looking east in the late 1930s. The popular Rohr's 5¢ to $1.00 Store is on the left.

start up a five cents to one dollar store similar to the one run by his father in Front Royal. Since money was tight, prices in his store made it popular. The arrival of the Dixie Theatre, the first movie house in town, provided a new source of entertainment. The theater had two narrow sections of four seats on each side of a center aisle. A pianist, either Eloise Trimmer Branch or her mother Mary Finley Compton, played the piano. Sometimes, records played on a Victrola provided background music.

By 1940, 1,302 residents called Manassas home. A town and county Chamber of Commerce organized in 1935. Natural gas service from Virginia Gas Distribution Corporation began in 1938. Rural electrification beyond the town limits spread quickly. The town gained its electricity from the Prince William Electric Cooperative.

Right: Groundbreaking for the new Central Mutual Telephone Company, 1957, on the corner of Lee Avenue and Peabody Street. Started in the early 1900s, in 1929 the phone company charged $3 a month for one line. C. Lacey Compton, Prince William County District Court judge (dark suit), holds the shovel.

Below: An outdoor gathering of the United Daughters of the Confederacy Manassas Chapter in 1949, possibly at the Manassas Battlefield for the anniversary of the First or Second Battle of Manassas. Organized in 1896, the chapter continues its public service and scholarships today.

Below: Pitt's Theatre, Main Street, in 1947 was advertised as "New Modern and Air Conditioned." Admission was ten cents for children and thirty-five cents plus tax for adults. *Gentlemen's Agreement* starring Dorothy McGuire and Gregory Peck won the Academy Award for best picture that year.

Right: Opening announcement from Rohr's 5¢ to $1.00 Store at 9126 Center Street. Opened by Edgar E. Rohr as an extension of his father's business in Front Royal, it sold a variety of items, and the second floor contained the first museum in Manassas. The business closed in 1997.

OPENING SALE

L. S. ROHR, INC.

5c to $1.00 STORE

MANASSAS Old Post Office Building, Battle Street VA.

FRIDAY & SATURDAY, AUG. 31, SEPT. 1

TENNIS SHOES 50c pr.

Aluminum Percolator 50c

MIXING BOWL 15c each

WASH PANS 10c

RAG RUGS 10c each

SALTED PEANUTS 10c lb.

DISH PANS 15c each

CUPS and SAUCERS $1 dozen

MIRRORS $1.00

APRONS 10c each

White Hand Bags 10c each

SALAD BOWLS 15c each

A few of our OPENING SPECIALS are listed in this advertisement. Be on Hand Friday and Saturday and get your share of these BIG BARGAINS

FUDGE 10c lb.

SANITARY NAPKINS 10c box

Men's Fancy Rayon SOCKS 10c pr

3 for 10c

DURELOUM MATS 10c each

THREAD 2c spool

TURKISH TOWELS 10c each

DUST MOPS 19c

ALARM CLOCKS

L. S. ROHR, INC.- 5c to $1.00 STORE

MANASSAS, VA.

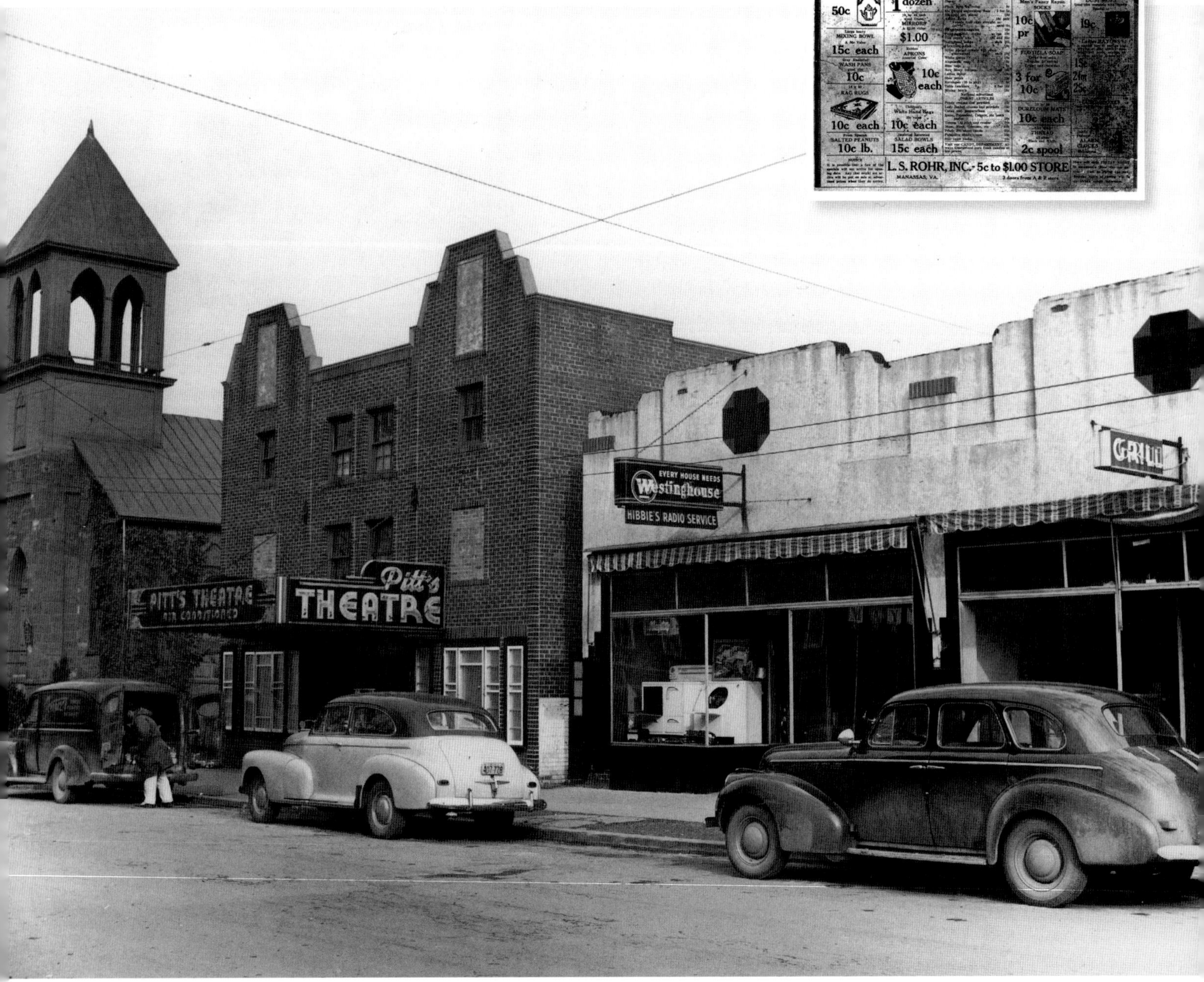

The abundance of multiple religious denominations with eleven churches within walking distance of the depot, regular railway transportation that ran through all major cities and towns between Maine and Manassas, and five reasonably priced hotels made Manassas a convenient location for quick marriages by out-of-towners. Licenses could be obtained at the Old Courthouse, within walking distance of the depot, for one dollar. The state did not require blood tests or waiting periods. There was even a visiting rabbi on some weekends. As war clouds once again hovered over Europe in the late 1930s, the number of young couples coming to town from eastern states increased substantially. Young men, fearing another draft, thought marriage might allow them exemption. In the 1940s, new state laws eliminated the easy rules that allowed most "quickie" marriages, and the influx lessened considerably.

Above: The Gregory Company at the corner of West and Center Street (possibly 9126 Center Street) advertised in the *Manassas Messenger* in 1945.

The early 1930s marriage of Anna Virginia Conner and Raymond Jackson Ratcliffe unified two well-known Manassas families. Presided over by Reverend A. S. Gibson of Trinity Episcopal Church, the reception at the Conner home on Main Street was not far from the Ratcliffe family home a few blocks away. Other young people who also married at this time included Frances Bushong and Sedrick Saunders, Arthur Sinclair and Ann Bradford, and Charles Walton Lewis and Lucy Arrington.

On a peaceful Sunday morning, December 7, 1941, citizens were jolted by the announcement of the bombing of Pearl Harbor. Many learned of the event as they left church. President Franklin Roosevelt

Left: Mary Susannah McDarment (1885–1984) made her home in Manassas after her wedding. She is wearing a 1910–1915 summer or tea dress decorated with a cameo, lace bodice, ribbons, and a trimmed overskirt of sheer material.

Vint Hill was an important communications station during World War II. On the eastern boundary of Fauquier County and Prince William County, on June 12, 1942, six months after the Japanese attack on Pearl Harbor, the Second Signal Service Battalion activated Vint Hill Farms Station as an Army Signal Security Agency monitoring station, performing signal intelligence, intercepts, communications, counterintelligence, and cryptography.

officially declared World War II the next day. Almost immediately, the entire state of Virginia saw radical changes. Northern Virginia saw construction of the Pentagon and the influx of multitudes of war support personnel into Washington, D.C. Closer to home, the Quantico Marine Base was reactivated and nearby Vint Hill began operation. In Manassas, many local men were drafted or volunteered. The Farquhar brothers, Butch, Charles, and William, John Geris, another generation of Johnson brothers, Paul Mitchell, Claude Albrite, James H. Payne, Edgar Rohr, and Harry Parrish were some of the local men who served. Before he could graduate from high school, Buddy Merchant found himself drafted and hitting the beach at Normandy.

The Red Cross and Civil Defense groups soon went into action. Local citizens watched for enemy planes from the Town Hall cupola or collected newspapers and tin cans for the war effort. Backyard Depression gardens soon became Victory Gardens. As gas rationing began, those who worked in Washington began the new custom of carpooling. Trains were used for transporting supplies and troops. Most people walked for local errands, parking their cars until the war ended. Blackout drills and ration cards for sugar, meat, coffee, shoes, and butter became commonplace. Civilian wardens patrolled the streets to ensure darkness at night. Women staged benefits such as plays or musical reviews to collect supplies and funds for the war effort and

Above: Future Farmers of America, 1948. Assembled in back of the Bennett School, the students are, left to right kneeling, John Robert Hooe Jr., Estel Yates, Tommy Fries, and Jack Barrett; left to right standing, Woodrow Hicks, Wayne Coverstone, Callie Stipe, Leon Kline, Harold Turner, Eddie Batonelette, Burt Roseberry, Gene Hurst, Alison Lund, Paige Beale, Chester Simpson, Elmer Plaster, and teacher Raymond Fishpaugh.

Above left: General Omar Bradley dines with servicemen at Vint Hill. General Bradley, commander of the D-Day ground forces, visited Vint Hill to personally deliver his thanks to the men and women involved, for serving, in his words, "so silently and yet so magnificently." Vint Hill continued to provide support to the Army in the years following World War II, including the Korean War, the Vietnam conflict, Grenada, Panama, and Operations Desert Shield and Storm. June 12, 1997, marked the closing of Vint Hill as an active installation.

Above right: Frank P. Browning Jr. of Manassas was an early enlistee into the Navy in World War II. His father, Fesick P. Browning, was a baggage agent for Southern Railway.

Above: Canning corn at the Manassas School Community Cannery. In 1944, the new cannery at Brentsville District High School at Nokesville served the entire county. Because of overcrowding there, Manassas applied to the State Board of Education, which provided $3,000. Manassas raised the additional $800 needed, and the Manassas cannery opened in 1945. Corn production was a significant part of the cannery output.

Above right: The Manassas School Community Cannery located behind Osbourn High School on Lee Avenue. At the end of 1946, approximately fifty thousand cans of vegetables, fruit, and meats were processed at Prince William County community canneries at Manassas, Occoquan, and Nokesville. According to the *Washington Post*, January 2, 1946, the canneries represent "one of the major advancements in the development of the county, which a recent survey shows second in the state in per capita income."

the Red Cross. Excess meats, poultry, and vegetables went overseas to feed the troops.

One of three county canneries was established in a building behind Manassas High School. People brought produce from their gardens to the cannery where, for a small fee, it was processed and sealed into tin cans. Cannery supervisors were paid from customer fees. This service lasted into the 1950s, until frozen food began to appear. The cannery building was also used for classroom overflow from the high school and 4-H Club meetings.

At the end of World War II, Manassas saw a flurry of marriages as soldiers returned. A post–World War II building boom resulted in development northward on Battle, West, Ewell, and Taylor streets and Grant Avenue. Subdivisions opened in Robnel, near Annaburg, and in Manassas Park.

Church weddings were major events for families. Pictured here are Herman and Clarabella Law, married on November 9, 1946 (left), and John and Angela Gregory, married June 6, 1948.

In 1947, the Church of God began their Summer Meetings west of town on Rixlew Drive. Open to all who wished to come, the camp could accommodate up to one thousand participants. National and international visitors plus local people often attend the daily and evening programs. The camp continues today and meets the week of July Fourth.

Young farmers returning from the war organized the Veterans' Farm Club to keep current with agricultural improvements. From a club-sponsored dairy show for the 4-H Club grew the notion of a county fair. Led by Joe Johnson of Clover Hill Farm, the fair began modestly in 1951 with two or three days in summer. As it grew, they erected tents and encouraged exhibits and contests for canned and baked

Five-year-old Bernard Clemen walks his sheep "Polly." Bernard was taking Polly shopping, showing her off to friends, and stopping traffic on the way to the 1955 Prince William County Fair.

A Golden Guernsey cow admires her cousins at the 1953 Prince William County Fair.

goods, and the highlight of the fair, livestock showing. To secure a permanent site for the ever-growing event, the fair group bought land south of town. Continuing every August, it now runs for two weeks and includes carnival rides, baby contests, and notable entertainers along with the traditional county fair exhibits and shows. Yearly attendance at the Prince William County Fair is now estimated to be more than ninety thousand, making it the state's largest fair.

The third child of twelve, Irving Jackson "Jack" Breeden entered the labor force when his father was killed in a Pittsburgh railroad explosion while laying track for the Wabash

Above: Longview Home Demonstration Club display at the 1952 County Fair.

Right: Prince William Farmers Service, November 1938, advertises Southern States Cooperative Motor Oil, feed, seeds, fertilizers, and Soya paint. Southern States was a pioneer in bulk feed delivery from their mills, and one of the first to tag all bags with feed specifications so farmers could identify all the ingredients.

Railroad. After serving in World War I, he was twenty-one years old when the war ended. He worked fifteen-hour days, saved his money, and started buying and refurbishing old houses in Washington, D.C., and Northern Virginia. Breeden rented the remodeled houses, covering the mortgage and making a profit. In 1928, speculating that a new bridge would be built over the Bull Run, he purchased most of the land between the Bull Run and Compton Road and built houses along Centreville Road (Route 28).

Within two years, Breeden discovered Manassas, married his second wife, Hilda Moser, and built a house for his family on West Street. In 1947, he purchased the Portner estate of three thousand acres, which covered acreage from Yorkshire into Manassas and west to Route 66. He remodeled Liberia mansion and made it his home. In 1953, he sold land to George Offutt and John Register, who built more than one thousand inexpensive Cape Cod–style homes in a subdivision they called Manassas Park. Some of this property was sold to Cecil Hylton, a former Centreville sod farmer, who built an additional eight hundred homes to the west; he called the subdivision Loch Lomond. In the early 1950s, Breeden developed the Manassas Shopping Center and built the Reb-Yank movie theatre on Mathis Avenue. Despite protests from the United Daughters of the Confederacy, he built a bowling alley on the site of the Civil War earthwork Fort Beauregard and apartments on the site of Robert Portner's former hunting preserve, which he named Deer Park subdivision.

Above: Manassas Service Station in the 1940s at the corner of Center and West streets. Between 1939 and 1943, the station had three owners, ending in 1943 with W. Caton Merchant, owner of Merchant's Tire and Auto Service. In the 1940s, immediate downtown Manassas had six service stations.

Middle: Union breastplate from the Civil War, found at Liberia Plantation in the 1950s. The Breedens allowed relic hunters to search their land, and the hunters often shared their finds with the family, who made a display box of the relics.

Left: Made from either maple or walnut, this American Empire dresser with a marble top is believed to have been in a second-floor bedroom at Liberia Plantation. The American Empire is an early nineteenth century design based on the French-inspired Neoclassical style.

These extensive developments put pressure on the limited road systems, especially on Sudley Road, which was then extended from Main Street to meet Centreville Road. In the 1960s, Breeden sold land in Manassas that became the Point of Woods subdivision. He sold Portner's Annaburg mansion to J. Kennedy Sills, who turned it into a nursing home affiliated with the new Prince William Hospital.

Above: William Harrison Lamb at work in his laboratory. He was editor of the *Manassas Journal* from 1929 to 1943 and wrote the definitive *Virginia Trees* in 1937. Upon his death, Mrs. Lamb became editor and ran the newspaper until 1945 when she sold it to Marshall Johnson of the Clover Hill Farm family.

The period between 1955 to 1973 was a period of great growth and expansion. Doctors John Ringler and Jessee Herald opened the first medical center on Centreville Road near

Right: Manassas Ice and Fuel Company, 1951. Edgar Goodloe Parrish and Truman R. Hurst purchased the company in 1923, and Parrish became the sole proprietor soon after. In the 1930s, Parrish also owned a gas station south of Manassas on Route 234. Edgar G. Parrish was on the Manassas Town Council from 1925 to 1947.

The late 1950s saw a six-man police force with headquarters in the Harry Parrish Town Hall. The Volunteer Fire Company, originally located there, moved into a new facility on Centreville Road. Left to right: Clarke E. Nalls, Luther Cox, Jack Dillon, Julian Hobbs, Charles Lyles, and Mr. Jones. The pay was slightly over $250 a month. There was no chief of police until 1961.

Sudley Road in 1951, which served the community until Prince William Hospital opened in 1964. The *Manassas Journal* and *Manassas Messenger* newspapers merged and publish now as the *News & Messenger*. In 1952, under the leadership of Ruth E. Lloyd and others in the Women's Club, the state granted funding of $22,612 for the first demonstration public library in Manassas. Today, in honor of her efforts, the Bull Run branch of the Prince William County Library System calls its Virginiana Room RELIC (Ruth E. Lloyd Information Center).

Georator Corporation opened for business in 1950, manufacturing electrical frequency converters and, more recently, electronic power supply converters. Retail businessmen organized the Retail Merchants Association. To keep pace with the ever-expanding housing developments, the volunteer fire department built a new firehouse on Centreville Road. Water, sewer, and electric power were also expanded to meet new demands. A local radio station, WPRW-AM Radio, began broadcasting in 1957. W. Caton Merchant began with one gas station and six tires in 1942, laying the foundation for the multimillion-dollar Merchant's Tire and Auto Centers that blanket today's Washington metro area.

Harry Warder was a quiet nineteen-year-old who seemed "strange" to many in town. He had an obsessive love of the actress Shirley Temple and publicly claimed he wanted to marry her. On March 18, 1950, her movie *Seabiscuit* came to town, showing at the new larger (Ben T.) Pitt's Theatre, a block down Main Street from the old Dixie Theatre. Warder had collected magazine articles about Temple, posted pictures on his bedroom walls, and purchased at least one 8 mm reel of a movie. The night of the showing of *Seabiscuit*, he went to the theatre and sat through two shows. After the movie, he hid in the closed theatre, went into the projection room, stole the film, and set fire to the theatre to hide his theft. It turned into a $50,000 blaze that threatened the business district and brought out nine fire companies. Later, when firemen answered a call to extinguish out a small fire in Warder's bedroom at home, they found the stolen film. He confessed to his crime and was sent to S. W. State Hospital in Marion, Virginia, for observation. Years later, Warder returned to Manassas to live a quiet and obscure life.

Paramount Pictures filming the movie *My Son John.* Nominated for an Oscar in Best Writing, it documents American culture of the early 1950s. The film chronicles the attempts of two All-American parents to save their son from the temptations of Communism.

In 1953, the county built a new Osbourn High School on Tudor Lane adjacent to South Main Street. Across the street was the new school board office. The new school considerably expanded classroom and gym space and had a sizeable football field, named later for James J. Leo. While working on the field, the construction crew discovered the iron casket of a young Confederate soldier killed during one of the Manassas battles. He was removed intact to the Confederate Cemetery on Center Street.

In the 1950s, Cocke Pharmacy was the focus for after-school socializing, and the Birmingham Milk Bar on Centreville Road near Prescott Avenue was busy on weekends. The milk bar served hamburgers, banana splits, and an orange drink called Green Spot. Many remember working as teenagers at Rohr's Store. While the pay was not spectacular, everyone in town shopped there, making it the center of commerce and activity.

Local girl Patty Lynn Adams (left), hoping for a Kodak moment with Helen Hayes and Dean Jagger, walks with them on West Street. Trinity Episcopal Church, where some filming took place, served meals to the cast and film crew.

An aerial view of Manassas with Clover Hill Farm in the foreground, circa 1960. (Photograph by Alton Marsh)

In March 1951, Paramount Pictures of Hollywood chose Manassas for the location in which to film the movie *My Son John*, to the excitement of much of the town. Filming took place at the W. L. Lloyd home on West Street. It starred Helen Hayes, Dean Jagger, Van Heflin, and Robert Walker. The patriotic theme dealt with Communism, the issue of the day, and was nominated for an Academy Award. Manassas Presbyterian Church hosted a church scene, and the Manassas Trinity Episcopal Church supplied food for the cast in its Parish Hall for which it received a $50 donation. Students were allowed out of school to watch an afternoon's filming. A premier opened on May 18, 1952, at a refurbished Pitt's Theatre. Prior to the showing, the Osbourn High School band marched through town and performed in front of the theatre.

Chapter VI
The Town Becomes a City
1953–Present

In the 1960s, Manassas laid the foundations upon which the modern twenty-first century city exists. Change and growth typified the last half of the twentieth century. Whereas one blinking light at the intersection of Center Street and Grant Avenue could control traffic in 1960, today every major intersection within the city's ten square miles has traffic lights. While Grant Avenue continues as two lanes lined with many trees similar to ones planted by George C. Round at the turn of the century, Sudley Road/234 and Centreville Road/28 have expanded to four lanes. Hoping to attract a younger population of homeowners to town, the first townhouse subdivision in the metro area, Georgetown South, began building in 1963. Built on a portion of the Johnson's Clover Hill Farm, this construction heralded a flood of new subdivisions over the next twenty years: Landmark Square, Point of Woods, Musket Hills, Hazel Ridge, Robnel, Cannon Ridge, and Owens Woods.

The 382-acre Clover Hill Farm was the last working farm within Manassas city limits in the 1970s. It had been in the Johnson family since 1770. Sold in 1987 to Northern Virginia developers Kettler & Scott, the land is bounded by Winters Branch, Clover Hill Road, Route 234 (Sudley Road), and the Manassas city line.

Despite the Supreme Court's decision in 1954 to desegregate public schools, the Commonwealth of Virginia resisted, and Prince

William County did not adopt a formal policy until the mid-1960s. The newest Osbourn High School on Tudor Lane and Jennie Dean High and Marsteller Middle School (named for Dr. Emlyn Marsteller) were integrated schools. The old African American high school, Manassas Institute, became an elementary school until "new" Bennett was completed in 1968. Eventually, that building was destroyed, and the original Bennett School housed the new county police force organized in the mid-1960s. While complying with desegregation, the county would never have succeeded without the perseverance of four black women, handpicked by Superintendent of Schools Stewart Beville to integrate as teachers into the traditionally white schools. In the spring of 1965, Fannie Fitzgerald and Maxine Coleman of Manassas were transferred within days: Fitzgerald was sent to Fred M. Lynn Middle and Elementary School; Coleman went to Featherstone Elementary. Since both were eastern county schools, they requested and received an extra $400 for gas. Also with only a few days' notice, Hazel Porter Sykes went to Dumfries Elementary and Zella Brown went to Loch Lomond Elementary. In the fall of 1965, administrators integrated all of the county schools, grades one through twelve, with both black and white students and teachers. Later, another black woman, Suella Ellis, was appointed assistant principal at Stonewall Jackson High School and, in 1980, principal of Osbourn Park High School in a career spanning forty-five years. Two county schools were named to honor Ellis and Fitzgerald for their roles in integrating the schools and providing leadership for their students.

Joseph B. Johnson (b. 1925) at Clover Hill Farm around 1960, with his purebred Jersey cows. Johnson preferred the Jersey cows because of the higher butterfat content of their milk but acknowledged that the high-volume Holstein cows were more popular with Prince William County dairy farmers.

In the 1960s, Johnson represented Manassas on the Prince William County Board of Supervisors. Later, when Manassas became a city in 1975, he was the first school board chair. (Birchfield Photo, courtesy of Jim Johnson)

Virginia moved slowly in making other changes to integrate the races. African Americans were a minority in Manassas, with about an 8 percent share of the population in the 1960s. African Americans' homes were, in essence, relegated to Liberty and Prince William streets, south of the railroad tracks. Although African Americans were free to spend money at white businesses on Center Street, they

Above: Desegregation of the public school system in Virginia took many years to accomplish. Two Prince William County African American women who were first to integrate schools were Maxine Coleman (top) and Fannie Fitzgerald (bottom). (Courtesy of *Manassas Journal Messenger*)

could not eat in the restaurants.

While federal action became necessary in some urban areas, in Manassas, however, two women, concerned about avoiding disruption, presented a plan for public accommodations for all.

Right: Dorothy Thomas (pictured) and Louise Brown were African Americans who worked with local civic leaders to integrate Manassas businesses in the 1960s.

Below: This freshmen class of 1931 at the Manassas Industrial School included Louise Brown (seated, on the left), who worked with Dorothy Thomas to integrate Manassas businesses.

In 1962, Louise Smith Brown, a county teacher, and Dorothy Gaskins Thomas, a U.S. government worker, developed a plan to peacefully desegregate public places. In a letter addressed to Dudley J. Martin, president of the Chamber of Commerce, Brown and Thomas requested a meeting with the Chamber to solve some of the social issues of the day. They were immediately invited to the next regular Chamber meeting at the integrated Lake Jackson Restaurant just outside of Manassas.

At the luncheon, five African American leaders met with twenty Chamber members. In an executive session that followed, the Chamber agreed to call a meeting the next week with owners of eating places to request desegregation of their facilities. After two hours' discussion, the restaurant owners decided that desegregation would be most effective if every owner acted immediately. Shortly thereafter, every other segregated public facility, such as the movie theatre, also desegregated.

In the 1960s, Prince William County became the fastest growing county in Virginia and in the nation as new housing seemed to sprout everywhere, especially in Manassas. The 1966 passage of a $5 million bond referendum by the town of Manassas enabled purchase of land on Broad Run in 1966 to construct a dam at Lake Manassas named for T. Nelson Elliott, town manager from 1953 to 1974. The dam provided water filtered through a newly built plant and carried seven miles underground by twenty-four-inch pipelines into storage tanks in town

Top: WPRW-AM 1460 was a local AM radio station with a directional antenna on Godwin Drive. Bluegrass DJ Red Shipley worked there from 1959 to 1966. The station carried local baseball games live, including those of the Manassas Lumberjacks.

Bottom: Center Street at Main Street, late 1950s. The building on the right at 9070 Center Street was the National Bank of Manassas, in 1896 the first bank to be established in Prince William County. It occupied this location from 1912 to 1956. In 1956, it became the First Virginia Bank.

Top: Civil War Centennial reenactment at the Manassas National Battlefield Park, 1961. The First Manassas Corporation, formed in March 1960 to support and plan a grand reenactment of the First Battle of Manassas, set the pattern for the next four years' commemorations. The corporation, with R. Jackson Ratcliffe as its president, staged a successful reenactment and ceremonies at the Manassas National Battlefield Park, attended by more than thirty thousand people. Intended to bolster American patriotism at the height of the cold war and boost tourism in the South, the national Civil War Centennial Commission saw pageants as an essential part of the commemoration. Many residents fondly recall the events celebrating America's triumph over division and strife.

Bottom: Annie Snyder (1902–2002), one of the Marine Corps' first female officers, was an outspoken activist who worked tirelessly for preservation. The first of what Mrs. Snyder called her many "battles of Manassas" to preserve the historic ground began in the 1950s when she successfully fought federal highway engineers who wanted to build an interstate through the middle of the battlefield. In the mid-1990s, she and other preservationists—most prominently the National Trust for Historic Preservation and historians David McCullough and Shelby Foote—worked to thwart Walt Disney's plans to build an American history theme park, housing, shops, and hotels on three thousand acres about four miles from the battlefield. In the mid-1990s, Mrs. Snyder launched the Save the Battlefield Coalition, and she and others convinced Congress to spend $120 million to buy land adjoining the battlefield, which saved the site from development.

to be dispensed to local customers. It joined the private Liberia plant by 1971 to serve the continuing annexation of land and new homes. The facility would be expanded in 1987. Eight wells continued to be kept available for backup. For Harry Parrish, who took office as mayor in 1963, this was a major accomplishment of his administration.

Along with the housing boom, new businesses arrived: the Earley Studio in 1962 and International Business Machines (IBM) in 1968. Within five years, IBM employed fifteen hundred people at its large Manassas campus. Center and Church streets changed to one-way traffic while Sudley Road expanded to four lanes.

Above: The 1963 Manassas Town Council, whose members were the last to serve under Mayor Harry P. Davis, who served for forty-two years. Left to right: back row: A. Stewart Vetter, Garnett Carpenter, James H. Payne, Robert Byrd, and Eugene Worley. Seated: Orrin Kline, Mayor Davis, and newly elected Mayor Harry Parrish.

To accommodate the influx of new people, the town assumed street maintenance, expanded the sewer system, and adjusted the town charter. By 1970, the population was close to nine thousand, demanding an expansion of representation on the five-member Town Council. The amended charter added two more seats on the council.

In 1959, Claude McLain, president of Birmingham Dairy, proposed the idea of a local hospital at a Kiwanis Club

Left: Aerial view of Manassas, 1973. With downtown in the lower center of the picture, it is clear that Manassas is expanding toward the airport in the upper right.

Harry J. Parrish was the second-longest serving mayor of Manassas. Born in Manassas, he was student government president and played sports at Manassas High School. Upon graduation, he attended Virginia Polytechnic Institute (now Virginia Tech) where he joined the Army Air Corps. Selected to represent the United States at the British Royal Air Force Flight School during World War II, he flew "the Hump" from India to China, supplying the Flying Tigers. A member of the Air Force Reserves, he flew special air missions during the Korean War and in and out of Saigon during the Vietnam War. Retiring as a colonel, Parrish received the Distinguished Flying Cross and the Presidential Unit Award.

In Manassas, Parrish chaired the board of the Manassas Ice and Fuel Company, serving in many organizations in conjunction with his business. In addition to being mayor, he was a council member, member of the Volunteer Fire Company, an original Prince William

Manassas Volunteer Fire Company in 1951, in front of their old headquarters, the Parrish Town Hall on Center Street. Founded in 1892, the company was the first fire department in Prince William County. In 2008, the City of Manassas created a Fire and Rescue Department. The department operates two stations, supporting four fire engines, one aerial ladder, one hazardous materials unit, one decontamination unit, four ambulances, two crash-rescue units, and one command unit. The Greater Manassas Volunteer Rescue Squad and the Manassas Volunteer Fire Company provide support for the department.

The Ladies Auxiliary to the Fire Company in 1954. Formed in 1952 to support the firefighters, the group evolved into a fundraising organization for the firehouse. Here they are in their new uniforms preparing to march in a dress parade in Orange, Virginia. They won first prize of $25.

Hospital board member, and a director of the Chamber of Commerce. At the state level, he was elected to the House of Delegates in 1992 representing Manassas, Manassas Park, and a portion of Prince William County, a position he held until his death in 2006. He was married to Mattie Hooe Cannon for sixty-two years. Prior to his death, he was honored by Manassas when the Old Town Hall was renamed Harry J. Parrish Town Hall. Their son, Harry J. Parrish II, was elected mayor of Manassas in 2008.

Above: Edgar Rohr, left, and Harry J. Parrish display an award presented to the city. Rohr was then mayor serving after Parrish, who became a delegate to the General Assembly in 1982, a position he held until his 2006 death.

Top left: The Volunteer Fire Company's new headquarters on Centerville Road in 1967. Ralph "Buddy" Moore stands near the latest fire engine.

Parrish Town Hall and City Hall decorated for the 2008 holidays. (Photograph by Larry Bates)

In 1964, Prince William Hospital opened its doors. It was made possible because citizens felt their growing community needed a hospital. Since then, it has been expanded to fill a fifty-five-acre campus and become the third-largest employer in the area. (Photograph by Don Flory)

meeting, noting that the closest hospital was more than thirty minutes away. The club agreed to promote for a hospital nearer to Manassas. To raise the money would be a phenomenal task for one organization, and soon the Lions Club embraced the idea as well. W. Caton Merchant became president of the board of directors of the hospital corporation and was tapped to serve as chair of the fundraising efforts. Serving until his death in 1975, Merchant helped raise $750,000 and more than $800,000 in pledges. A federal grant of $790,900 in matching funds allowed construction to begin. In 1962, the Woman's Club stepped in to help fundraising and begin the hospital auxiliary with charter members Angela Gregory and Nancy Parrish Lawson.

The auxiliary initially raised $5,000 annually. Today through their hospital gift shop, Old Town Thrift Shop, and annual bazaars, they raise upwards of $275,000 a year for the hospital.

Thus, the Prince William Hospital had very strong local support when it opened its doors in 1964. As the population continued to grow, so too did the hospital. By 2004, it filled a fifty-five-acre campus and was the area's third largest employer. Nearly four hundred physicians in forty-one specialties practice in the area. Most recent additions have been a birthing center, an ambulatory surgery center, an upgraded emergency department, and outreach branches to include a nursing facility and a smaller branch hospital in Haymarket.

Joe Hyde's Heath Parasol monoplane at the first Manassas Airport, 1936. Pilot Francis B. Compton flew this plane, possibly built by Joe Hyde. During the late 1920s and early 1930s, the Parasol was the only airplane that could be constructed at home from a factory-built kit and be licensed by the FAA. The Heath was extremely popular, being economical to build and operate, and easy to fly.

Alvin E. Conner, the first pediatrician to practice in Prince William County, was born to Jacob K. Conner and Virginia H. Conner in 1924. The family of ten had a farm on Lucasville Road. Conner graduated from Manassas High School, served for two years in the army medical corps, and was stationed at Liege, Belgium, during the Battle of the Bulge in World War II. This experience led him to attend the Medical College of Virginia (MCV) after graduating from Bridgewater College. He began his medical practice as a general practitioner but returned to MCV to complete his residency in pediatrics.

Upon returning to the Manassas area, Conner found himself making house calls throughout the county, even traveling as far as Culpeper. Eventually, he took on several partners and established the Pediatrics Association of Manassas to meet the needs of the ever-growing community. In 1959, he was one of thirteen physicians who formed the Prince William Medical Society and served as its first president. From 1959 to 1964, Dr. Conner was a member of the Medical Advisory Committee to establish Prince William Hospital. In 1966, he served as president of the Prince William Medical Staff and later as chairman of the pediatric department.

In addition to his varied medical activities, Conner was active in the Manassas Church of the Brethren and served on the Board of Directors of the Didlake School for Mentally Retarded, the Manassas City School Board, and the Commonwealth Saving and Loan Bank Board. He and his wife raised two children while his practice flourished in Manassas.

Charles "Chuck" Joseph Colgan (b. 1926) at the Manassas Regional Airport in 1985. He founded Colgan Airways Corporation at Manassas Airport in 1965. In 1970, it began scheduled service under contract with IBM between Manassas, Washington, D.C., and Poughkeepsie, New York. It expanded over the next decade and a half and was sold in 1986 to Presidential Airways. A Democrat, Colgan was elected to the Senate of Virginia in 1975. He currently is president *pro tempore* of the Virginia Senate, and the longest-serving member of the Senate.

Along with expanded roads, health care, and schools, Manassas needed a larger airport. By the early 1960s, increasing traffic on Sudley Road/234 and the growing number of businesses on the western corridor forced out the Sudley Road airport. Four miles west of downtown, the Town of Manassas purchased 250 acres from Benjamin O. Wakeman on which to build a new airport, complete in 1964. Before long, Colgan Airways, owned by Charles Colgan, a World War II veteran aviator, began a flight school and private service for IBM employees to their home base in Poughkeepsie, New York.

Most of these ventures pushed the fringes of town, requiring Town Council to annex county land to the west and south. A 1957 annexation of 899.3 acres filled up, and the town then wanted to annex land to include

IBM, the airport, the hospital, and Woodbridge Clay properties within its borders. Appeals by Prince William County, which feared the loss of tax revenue, were rebuffed by the courts, and on December 5, 1970, the town tripled in size to its present ten square miles. With plenty of expansion room, the population could and did soar: 9,164 in 1970; 15,438 in 1980; 27,957 in 1990; 35,135 in 2000; and 36,638 in 2006.

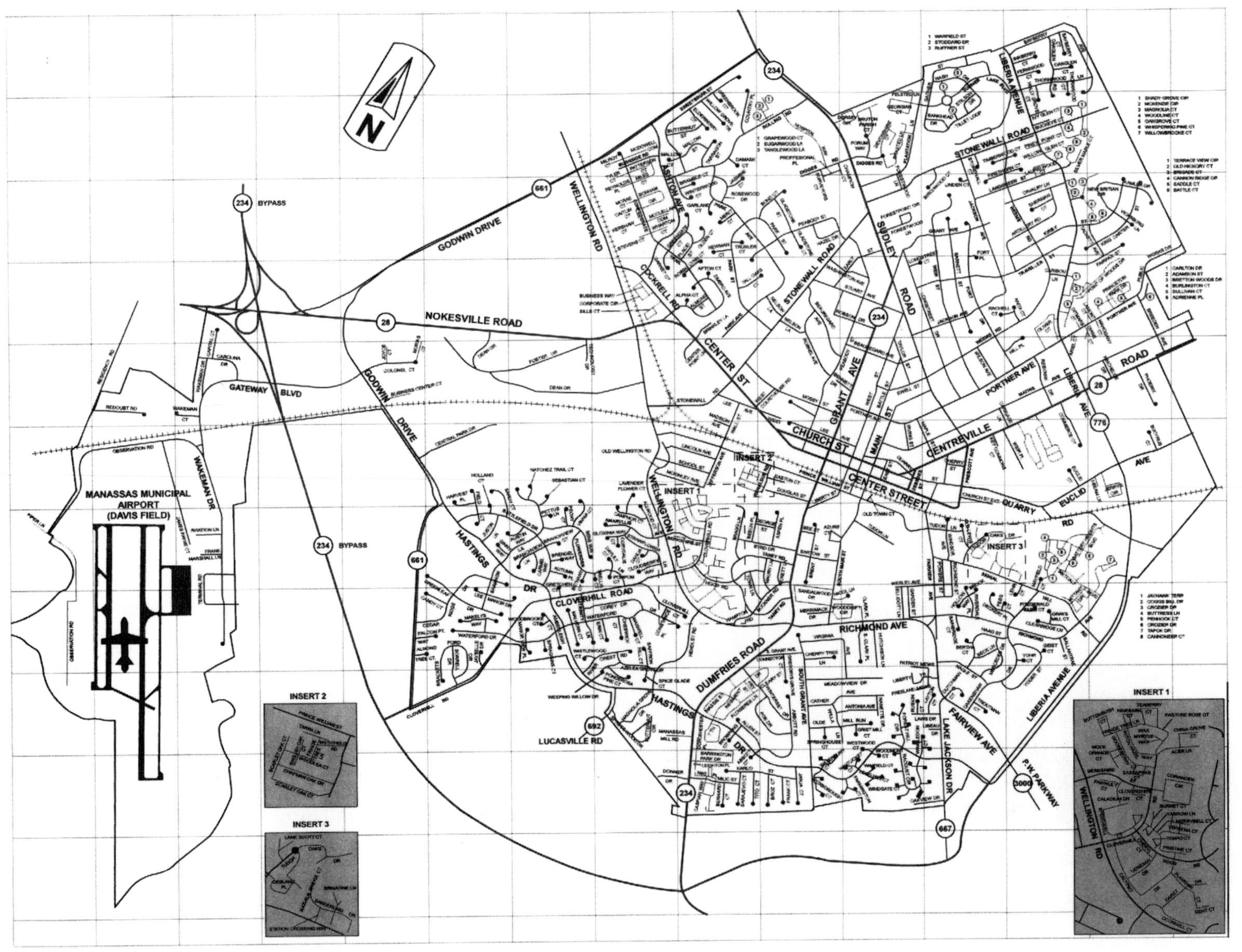

City of Manassas map, September 2008. (GIS/Mapping, City of Manassas)

Right: Smitherwood in 1984—the last significant piece of undeveloped land in the city of Manassas before it was turned into a subdivision. The ninety-three-acre parcel was owned by Judge Selwyn and Virginia Smith and family and sold to the Ariston Group in 1999.

To meet public safety demands, in 1972 the police department moved out of Town Hall into a separate building on Fairview Avenue. By the 1980s, Town Hall had become overcrowded, and plans were underway to build a new facility nearby. City Hall was completed in 1988.

Growth in the 1980s and 1990s tended toward the southeastern part of the city, including the Oakenshaw, Baldwin Oaks, Owens Brooke, and Battery Heights developments. The remaining land from the Clover Hill Farm became Wellington in the southwestern part of town. The final subdivision to complete major housing build out in Manassas started in 2001 when Judge Selwyn Smith sold his property to become the Summer Lake development in the northwest corner of the city.

In 1973, Manassas celebrated its centennial as a town with a gigantic six-day celebration. A Centennial Committee was organized and contracted the John B. Rogers Producing Company of Fostoria, Ohio, to help plan festivities. The celebration, with activities for all ages, ran from June 28 through July 3, 1973. Sidewalk and storefront displays highlighted town history. Garden Club members led tours of older homes in town. The parade down Center Street highlighted all generations. Salutes to all the churches and fraternal and patriotic organizations occurred. Stores held Old Fashioned Bargain Days. Southern Railway sent an exhibit car displaying various aspects of railway operations. A Celebration Dinner and Ball honored selected dead and living outstanding men and women in town history. Deceased honorees were George C. Round and Jennie

Below: Jim Syring in June 1995. In 1991, assisted by friends and the Lake Jackson Garden Club, he planted a collection of old roses at Smitherwood. When he learned that Smitherwood was to be sold, he gave the rose collection to the garden club. The club relocated the roses to the sunny, fertile grounds of the county's historic Ben Lomond House on Sudley Manor Drive in Manassas. They moved two hundred roses in two days.

Left: The "new" Rohr's 5¢ to a $1 Store at the corner of Center and West streets as it appeared in 1948.

Below left: With shelves overflowing with notions, toys, penny candy, housewares, and more, Rohr's was a downtown attraction as well as a shopping experience.

Below right: The first Manassas Museum on Main Street was opened in 1974.

The A & P Grocery store at 9136 Mathis Avenue near Sudley Road and the Manassas Shopping Center were built by I. J. Breeden. The lot was most recently occupied by Patriot Bank.

Dean. Living honorees were Harry Parrish and Walser Rohr.

Walser Conner Rohr gathered a collection of artifacts from local residents to illustrate Manassas' first hundred years and displayed them on the second floor of today's Fauquier Bank at the corner of Center and Main streets. The artifacts became the nucleus for the Manassas Museum. Inspired by the Manassas Centennial, local citizens slowly awakened to value their history and wanted to preserve it. The next year, 1974, the original National Bank building on Main Street was purchased by the Historical Commission and dedicated as a museum.

The Women's Club sponsored an oil painting of George C. Round accompanied by a biography written by Rita G. Koman. The painting hung prominently in the new museum. Ren Conner, the curator, and volunteers put a museum together, open on Saturdays to the public. As part of the national bicentennial celebration in 1976, the museum was formally dedicated. The first full-time director/curator, Douglas Harvey, began in 1982.

Population growth signaled the need for yet another change. In 1973, Manassas decided to become a city. This move, anticipated for a number of years, was accelerated by double shifts at the local high school and overcrowded classrooms in other town schools. By establishing its own school system, Manassas knew it could control the system itself and would no longer have to accede to county decisions and fight for county funding. The new district purchased and remodeled Osbourn High School, Dean Middle School, and Baldwin Elementary School from Prince William County. The city then built Weems Elementary. All these schools opened as city schools in the fall of 1977 with James J. Leo serving as superintendent.

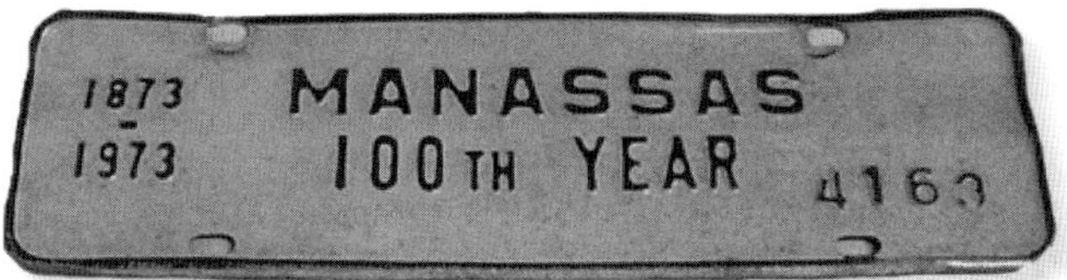

A World War II veteran, Mr. Leo began his career as teacher and coach at Osbourn High School in 1945, followed by positions as assistant principal and principal of other county schools. Working with an office staff of three, he administered a $5.2 million budget to start the new city school system and retired in 1983.

Within a few years, the county moved its school board offices to Independent Hill, and the city took over the Tudor Lane facility for its first school board headed by Joe Johnson. When Osbourn High School opened its doors in the fall of 1977, Victor Egidi was principal and L. A. Roherrer was assistant principal. In 2008, the newest school's commons area was named to honor these men for their leadership in starting up the high school. Hayden Elementary School opened in 1978, followed by Round Elementary School in 1986. By the 1990s, Dean became an expanded elementary school and Metz Middle School was built. By 2005, the old Osbourn High School was completely replaced. In 2006, Mayfield Intermediate School for fifth and sixth graders opened.

Above: Mae S. Merchant, widow of W. Caton Merchant, founder of Manassas-based Merchant's Inc. Mrs. Merchant's philanthropy has benefited arts and culture in the Manassas area. In 1998, the Merchant family donated the proceeds from two trusts to expand the Manassas Museum and also donated the Hopkins Candy Factory building to the City of Manassas to house the Center for the Arts. Mrs. Merchant is shown here on the steps of her Grant Avenue home during a benefit tea for the museum in the 1990s.

Above left: The City of Manassas issued metal car tax tags for proof of taxes paid. This is the 1973 tag commemorating the City of Manassas Centennial (1873–1973).

Left: The Manassas Volunteer Fire Company, 1977. Their fleet of equipment is on display in front of the firehouse on Center Street.

On November 8, 1999, the students and staff moved only a few feet from the old Osbourn to the new Osbourn High School at 9005 Tudor Lane. The science wing from the 1980s was renovated to house the Johnson Learning Center and is now a free-standing building. (Photograph by Don Flory)

Lillian Orlich is the longest-serving employee of the Prince William County School District and a Manassas resident since 1950. Arriving from New York State at age twenty-two, she first taught world history and English at the original Osbourn High School on Lee Avenue. On November 1, 1953, the faculty and two hundred students moved into a new building on Tudor Lane. Orlich earned $2,000 as a beginning teacher and lived well on that salary in Manassas. Living first in Old Town, she walked to and from school daily. There was only one other high school at the time—Garfield in the eastern end of the county. In 2009, two other county high schools and Manassas Park High School surround the newest Osbourn High School. In 1970, Orlich became a guidance counselor, a role she still performs at Osbourn Park High School. Her students have included mayors, a professional basketball player, judges, generals, and many young people over the years. Retirement is NOT in her vocabulary!

In the 1970s, the City Recreation and Parks Department formed to develop parks and other amenities for citizens. Stonewall Park and Pool, followed by Nelson Park, named for Mr. and Mrs. C. P. Nelson, and Jennie Dean Park were the first facilities. Up until this time, residents could only purchase membership in the private Sudley Pool and Tennis Club located on Rixlew Lane. Population growth and increased homebuilding attracted more business development within the city limits and in the nearby county. Shopping centers, like Manassas Junction, the Manassas Mall, Manaport, and Westgate, sprouted along Routes 28 and 234. The Manassas campus of Northern Virginia Community College opened in the early 1970s near the Manassas National Battlefield.

The oldest section of the city was set apart as a National Historic District in 1979 to protect its integrity. In 1984, the local Old Town Historic

District was officially designated, and in 1985, Historic Manassas Inc. organized the first Main Street Project sponsored by the National Trust for Historic Preservation. Planned to stimulate economic vitality and fill up Old Town's vacant storefronts to compete with shopping centers sprawled west of the city, a network of local business people, spearheaded by Loy E. Harris, began to rehabilitate Old Town. With federal and state tax incentives contingent on carefully rehabilitating the historic structures to preserve them, Harris began by buying one building, restoring it, and moving on to another. Soon others followed his lead, and within a few years, new businesses appeared. Restaurants opened along with new specialty shops. Sidewalks were widened, crosswalks were made user-friendly, and benches were strategically placed along Center Street. In 1988, the Old Town Historic District was placed on the National Register of Historic Places.

Above: The Manassas team from the ABC television show *Almost Anything Goes*. Each week, three teams (each representing a town in the United States and consisting of members from the town) competed for money and prizes. The competitions varied from week to week and included bizarre obstacle courses, pie throwing contests, swing relays, and other humorous events. In 1974 or 1975, the Manassas team competed against Culpeper. Left to right: James Rothrock, Patty Sawyer, Cindy Wall, Gretchen Day, Glendell Hill, Mike Martin, Randy Lee, Linda Womack, and J. L. "Nick" Niccolls.

Left: The gazebo in Nelson Park under a snowfall with traffic at the Grant Avenue light. Several newer homes have been built on Grant Avenue near this intersection with Sudley Road. (Photograph by Beverly Humphreys)

Above: The Loy E. Harris Pavilion, 9201 Center Street, shown here in 2008, is used in winter for ice skating and at other times for concerts, shows, and the Old Town Farmers' Market. As recently as 1995, thirty-three buildings were vacant in Old Town. It was during that year that Loy E. Harris (1942–1999), a local insurance broker, opened his Opera House Gourmet downtown. Harris soon purchased more buildings in the area. Other business leaders followed his example, transforming Old Town into a lively historic district with a variety of businesses. (Photograph by Larry Bates)

Right: Manassas City Council, 1984. The council met on the second floor of Harry Parrish Town Hall until the new city hall was built. Left to right: Maury Gerson; Richard Byrd Jr.; A. Stewart Vetter; Ralph Moore, city clerk; Mayor Edgar E. Rohr; James H. Payne; Louise Galleher; John Weber; and C. M. Moyer Jr., city manager.

50th

Anniversary
Calendar

1936 – 1986

Thank You For Your Patronage
We Appreciate Your Business
J.E. Rice

Above left: The cover of J. E. Rice's fiftieth anniversary calendar. Rice started in 1936 with a Western Auto associate store at the corner of East and Center streets and opened another store at the Manassas Shopping Center in 1958. The Rice family continues to operate the second store there, passing management to the next Rice generation.

Above right: Johnson "Fat Cat" McRee (1923–1990) and band at the Manassas Jazz Festival in 1987. Johnson began the Manassas Jazz Festival in 1966, taking his inspiration from the Manassas Kiwanis Club's "Kiwanis Capers" minstrel shows. As an investor in the famous Blues Alley in Washington, D.C., he had access to some of the world's best performers and brought them to Manassas. He produced more than 125 albums and 75 radio programs. The festival ran until 1989. Left to right: ———, "Wild Bill" Davison on trumpet, Tommy Saunders on trumpet (or cornet), Mason "Country" Thomas on clarinet, and Johnson on vocals. (Photograph © Michael Wilderman/JazzVisionsPhotos.com)

Orville and Mabel "Granny" Hersch opened their farm near Godwin Drive to elementary school children for field trips. Orville delighted in showing the eggs, goats, and rabbits, and he enjoyed giving tours around the farm and getting people involved with the animals and the activities. After Orville passed away in 1984, Mabel continued to welcome visitors to the Fun Farm, inviting them to help her gather eggs, spread freshly cut apples through the house to dry, touch Tinker the cow, and help in her garden. Granny Hersch never charged admission. After she passed away in 1987, a generous portion of the Hersch estate was left to Heifer International and became the Orville and Mabel Harley Hersch Education Endowment.

Above: Construction below the tracks on Grant Avenue in 1984. The influx of citizens and businesses created traffic congestion throughout the business district whenever a train arrived. Addition of the Grant Avenue Railroad Overpass and changing Center and Church streets to one-way in opposite directions relieved some of the pressure.

Above right: The new Manassas City Hall entrance, completed in 1990, is at 9027 Center Street, adjacent to the Harry Parrish Hall. A free-standing four-story building, described by then-city manager Macon Sammons, "with the landmark quality that a city hall should have." (Photograph by Larry Bates)

Right: Built in 1902 by H. Thornton Davies, a commonwealth's attorney from 1901 to sometime after the 1920s, this landmark home located at 9250 Bennett Drive was expanded in the 1960s by Robert and Helen Bridges. (Photograph by Don Flory)

Nineteen eighty-five saw the completion of the underpass on Grant Avenue beneath the Norfolk Southern railroad tracks. With a generous donation from the city, the new Judiciary Center and regional jail, a shared regional facility with the county and Manassas Park, opened in 1984. In 2008, a sizeable addition was made to the jail. The 1892 county courthouse was refurbished as a county historic site and reopened to house the county clerk's office and provide room for meetings and events. Manassas was now the fastest growing city in Virginia.

After an economic downturn initiated by IBM's exodus in 1988, circumstances began improving in the early 1990s. Defense contractor Lockheed Martin and Dominion Semiconductor, a joint Toshiba-IBM venture in computer chip production, arrived. City Council pushed for broader development at the airport's Gateway Business Park, and revitalization of Old Town took shape. In 1992, the Virginia Railway Express (VRE) launched a commuter rail service to Alexandria and Washington, D.C., with a stop at Manassas and at Broad Run. With capacity ridership filling seventy-two cars on multiple runs by 2002, VRE had to buy new double-decker cars. In 1997, the train depot, long the city's historic symbol, was refurbished and now serves more than eighty thousand commuters and visitors a year. The Hopkins Candy Factory, given to the city by the Merchant family, underwent a $2.5 million restoration that rehabilitated its exterior and interior to house the Prince William Center for the Arts.

In a 2002 appraisal of Manassas, then mayor Marvin Gillum, a native who grew up on Grant Avenue, proudly expounded upon the city's economic growth, completion of the Route 234 bypass around the city, and the VRE as a carrier of twelve thousand regular passengers.

Top: Amtrack and Virginia Railway Express serve more than seventy-five thousand trips a year out of the Manassas depot. Commuters travel to points east, into Union Station in Washington, D.C., and then home again.

Bottom: The Hopkins Candy Factory after renovation by the city. Historic signs "Manassas Feed and Milling" and "Millers and Wholesale Feed Dealers" represent the area's agricultural heritage and the varied uses of the building over time. (Photograph by Larry Bates)

He further cited the phenomenal Prince William Health/Hospital System under continual expansion, the Manassas Regional Airport, the largest general airport in Virginia with more than 150,000 takeoffs and landings annually, and the city police department under Chief John Skinner, which is among the 2–3 percent nationally that is fully accredited. Other assets for the city include the opening of the Prince William Branch of George Mason University, the Freedom Aquatic Center, and the expansion of Northern Virginia Community College's Manassas Campus located next to the Manassas National Battlefield Park.

Perhaps the best advantages the city has to offer its diverse population, now including many Asian and Hispanic families, are cultural and recreational.

The Judicial Center for Prince William County, Manassas, and Manassas Park at 9311 Lee Avenue. Built in 1984 at a cost of $10 million, costs for the 129,000-square-foot structure were split, with Prince William County paying 76.1 percent; City of Manassas, 20 percent; and City of Manassas Park, 3.9 percent. In 2002, the Center underwent a $9 million expansion and upgrade that increased its size by another 48,000 square feet. (Photograph by Larry Bates)

Manassas Veterans' Memorial, 2008. Located on Main Street beside the Manassas Museum, the memorial was dedicated on Memorial Day 2004. "Dedicated in honor and in memory of those who fought, those who served, and those who fell. Freedom is not free." (Photograph by Allan Kaufman)

The Manassas Museum System has eight properties under its jurisdiction: the Manassas Museum, Manassas Industrial School/Jennie Dean Memorial, Mayfield and Cannon Branch earthwork fortifications, Liberia Plantation, the Southern Railway Depot, the Hopkins Candy Factory, and the Speiden Carper House. Opened in 2001, the Loy E. Harris Pavilion and City Square provides space year-round for social activities of ice skating, band concerts, public fair days, various music concerts, some with dancing, and a summer farmers market. Little League ball parks abound throughout the city, and swimming pools are located in several areas. In 2007, the Boys and Girls Club opened next to Jennie Dean Elementary School. The George Mason University Hylton Performing Arts Center began construction in 2008 west of town on the university's Prince William campus and will expand local entertainment possibilities when completed in 2010. New and expanded businesses continue to contribute to the city's growing economic base. The largest business operating in Manassas in 2009 was Micron Technology, which employs twenty-one thousand, while Lockheed Martin was second with eighteen thousand employees.

Old Town's revitalization is evolving, continually challenging the Old Town businesses to remain viable during variable economic times and maintain its rich historical atmosphere. Old Town has sparked continuing economic development within other areas of the city. Liberia Avenue beyond the Battery Heights development hosts Signal Hill Shopping Center and

Above left: Cocke Pharmacy (1919–1984) was a popular site for after-school cherry Cokes and social life. Built between 1885 and 1895, the Art Deco building front has been altered until much of the original design has disappeared. The brick wall that fronts Battle Street is laid in six-course American bond, and until recently, a painting displayed historic advertisements from the mid-twentieth century. The star-shaped tie rods that hold the building's lateral braces are still visible.

Above right: A 2008 view of Grant Avenue looking north. Some of the oldest buildings in the historic district are scattered along Grant Avenue. Soon after it was opened to development in the 1890s, upper-middle class residents built Queen Anne–style dwellings there. (Photograph by Larry Bates)

Above: Manassas Gateway Business Park is a seventy-five-acre mixed-use tract owned by the City of Manassas. Adjacent to the Manassas Regional Airport, it is expected to have a range of commercial tenants. The forested area in the lower right is Cannon Branch Civil War Earthwork Park. (Photograph by Roger Snyder, retired director of Community Development, City of Manassas)

Top: The Manassas Museum is decorated for annual lighting of the Community Christmas Tree on the museum lawn, December 2008. (Photograph by Larry Bates)

Davis Ford Crossing Shopping Center, with others on the drawing board. The limitation on outward expansion has forced the newest additions within the city limits to rise three to five stories in various places surrounding the historic district such as the Vanderpool and RE/MAX Olympic buildings on Church Street near Grant Avenue. The Manassas Regional Airport business park lists more than thirty businesses in its 2009 directory. Nearby is the Northern Virginia branch of Farmville's Green Front Furniture Company.

In 2006, all Virginians learned where Manassas is located when Osbourn High School's football coach Steve Schultze led his undefeated team to a first-time state championship. In late summer 2008, a public parking building for more than four hundred cars was completed on Prince William Street across from the museum. The city remains vibrant as more people discover it. Special events can draw as many as two hundred thousand people a year to Old Town. These community events include the Heritage Railway Festival, the Jazz Festival, a fireworks extravaganza on July Fourth, the October Fall Jubilee, and the Christmas parade in December. This ever-changing historic community continues to be recreated by its citizenry.

Left: The Manassas City Council in early 2009, seated, from left to right: J. Steven Randolph, Mayor Harry J. Parrish II, and Vice Mayor Andrew L. Harrover; back row, from left to right: Marc T. Aveni, Jonathan L. Way, Mark D. Wolfe, and Steven S. Smith.

Below: Osbourn Eagles, the high school's 2006 undefeated football team with a 14–0 record. The Eagles finished their season with a 42–20 win over Chantilly, making them Virginia AAA Division 6 Champions. About 9,500 fans attended the game. Steve Schultze, a 1980 Osbourn graduate, was their coach. (Photograph by Dave Dillinger)

Osbourn Senior High School
2006 State Champions
Virginia AAA, Division 6

On August 11, 1870, Walter Weir, thirty-one, was buried in the Liberia family cemetery, and on September 26, 1989, he was "resurrected." A lieutenant in the Forty-ninth Virginia Infantry, Weir fought in both Manassas battles. His mother, Harriet, gave water to men of both sides on the battlefield. A graduate of William and Mary, he died from an abscessed tooth, leaving his wife Joan and young daughter Julie to mourn him. While the elder Weirs suffered financially because of the war, they apparently had recovered to a certain degree by the time of his death because they interred Walter in a very expensive cast iron coffin with a glass viewing window. Little attention was paid to the cemetery until his coffin and others were unearthed to make way for a condominium complex parking lot. To relocate him and the others buried there closer to the family home of Liberia, all known relatives granted their permission. Thus, they rediscovered Walter at his "resurrection."

Most significantly for scientists, anthropologists, and archeologists, his remains were still largely intact, allowing for careful scrutiny. Scientists studied the antibodies in his bones and learned information about every disease he ever had. Smithsonian forensic anthropologist Doug Owsley noted that bones reflect everything a person has done in life, and the groundbreaking techniques developed to study Weir's bone marrow would be used in the future on ancient corpses throughout the world. The casket itself was made by Crane and Breed Coffins of New Jersey and is only the third of its kind unearthed in the United States.

Above left: Liberia, 1975. The Breedens did not continue dairy farming on the parcel, but lived in Liberia and made some changes to the exterior of the house and property. A two-story Greek Revival–style porch, extending the length of the façade, significantly changed the appearance of Liberia. In 1986, the Breeden family donated the house and associated property to the City of Manassas.

Left: Liberia Plantation about 1900. The Liberia property remained a dairy operation for over 50 years under Portner family ownership. Additional quarters, dairy barns, and outbuildings were constructed on the property to support tenant farming operations. The Liberia house was occupied by two farm managers and their families until the property, about nineteen hundred acres, was sold by Portner to I. J. and Hilda Breeden in 1947. Portions of the property around the house were sold and subsequently developed as housing communities.

The popularity of the little museum on Main Street and the availability of more artifacts depicting life in both the city and nearby county led city council to build a new, larger facility on the Isaac Baldwin property on Prince William Street. Completed in 1991, the Manassas Museum soon became a popular site to visit. The new facility established an education program that quickly caught on with local schools.

The Museum System is supported by the city with a staff and volunteers, as well as support from the Manassas Museum Associates. Besides the permanent gallery, changing exhibits highlight various aspects of local history. A rich archive of books and artifacts is added to regularly through membership and donations. Year-round educational programs engage students of all ages. Echoes, a well-stocked museum store, entices many visitors.

The Manassas Museum on Prince William Street just after completion in 1991. The museum opened in 1974 at 9366 Main Street but shortly outgrew that location. In 1987, the Museum Committee and City Council selected the Baldwin Park site.

Above: One hundred three years after the fire of 1905, businesses on the north side of the railroad tracks now have a West Street address. They are Foster's Grille, The Things I Love, and City Square Café. The Depot is on the south side of the tracks. (Photograph by Larry Bates)

Left: A downtown lamppost decorated for the winter holidays welcomes everyone to Merry Old Town. (Photograph by Larry Bates)

City of Manassas National Register of Historic Places

Liberia Plantation
8601 Portner Avenue

Entered on the National Register of Historic Places on March 20, 1980
Virginia Department of Historic Resources #155-0001

Harriett Bladen Mitchell Weir and her husband William James Weir built their distinctive brick house on a plantation they named "Liberia" in 1825. By July 1861, the house served as the headquarters for General P. G. T. Beauregard, CSA. Some reports record its use as a hospital after the First Battle of Manassas and that Beauregard received his battlefield promotion from CSA President Jefferson Davis here. A year later, the Weirs fled Liberia. General McDowell, USA, occupied the house in the spring of 1862 for his military headquarters. It was during this period that President Abraham Lincoln came to Liberia to confer with his generals.

Manassas National Register Historic District

Entered on the National Register of Historic Places on June 29, 1988
Virginia Department of Historic Resources #155-0161

Includes the downtown core, east to Fairview Avenue, west to portions of Grant Avenue, north to Beauregard Avenue, and south to the railroad track.

Manassas Industrial School/Jennie Dean Memorial
9601 Wellington Road

Entered on the National Register of Historic Places on August 1, 1994
Virginia Department of Historic Resources #155-0010

After decades of fundraising by Jennie Serepta Dean, a former slave, the Manassas Industrial School for Colored Youth opened on October 7, 1893. The school was designed as a private residential institution providing both academic and vocational training within a Christian setting. Enrollment quickly grew to over 150. Students paid tuition or worked off their fees. Modeled after Booker T. Washington's approach, schools like these were the only way a child of a former slave might obtain a higher education.

Cannon Branch Fort
10509 Wakeman Drive

Entered on the National Register of Historic Places on August 26, 1999
Virginia Department of Historic Resources #155-5020

The location of Cannon Branch Fort indicates that it was one of the earthworks built under the orders of Union General George G. Meade in the fall of 1862. It is positioned at the point where the Orange & Alexandria Railroad crossed a stream known as Cannon Branch. The size of the fort suggests it would have held a company of federal troops and perhaps several cannon.

Mayfield Fortification
8401 Quarry Road

Entered on the National Register of Historic Places on August 8, 1989
Virginia Department of Historic Resources #155-5002

The defenses of Manassas were constructed in 1861 by Confederate General P. G. T. Beauregard in less than three months. The easternmost earthen fort was built at Mayfield, a farm owned by the Hooe family since the eighteenth century. Union General George B. McClellan's decision in 1862 not to attack Manassas Junction defenses head-on was justified by interpreting the forts as impregnable. Little did he know that Mayfield and other forts were armed with "Quaker guns," or logs carved and painted to look like cannon.

Select Bibliography

Bushong, Gladys. Personal Papers and Articles, 1950s and 1960s.

Evans, D'Anne. *Prince William County: A Pictorial History.* Virginia Beach, Va.: Donning Co., 1989.

Ewell, Alice Maude. *A Virginia Scene or Life in Old Prince William.* Lynchburg, Va.: J. P. Bell Company, Inc., 1931.

Galke, Laura J., ed. *Cultural Resource Survey and Inventory of a War-Torn Landscape: The Stuart's Hill Tract, Manassas Battlefield Park, Virginia.* Washington, D.C.: National Park Service, 1992.

Harris, Scott. National Register of Historic Places Application Form for Manassas Historic District Status. Manassas, Va.: Manassas Museum System, 1999.

Harrison, Fairfax. *Landmarks of Old Prince William: A Study of Origins in Northern Virginia,* 2nd reprint ed. Baltimore: Gateway Press, 1987.

Hennessy, John J. *The First Battle of Manassas: An End to Innocence, July 18–21, 1861.* Lynchburg, Va.: H. E. Howard, Inc., 1989.

———. *Return to Bull Run: The Campaign and Battle of Second Manassas.* Norman: University of Oklahoma Press, 1999.

Johnson, Elizabeth Harrover, E. R. Connor III, and Mary Harrover Ferguson. *History in a Horseshoe Curve,* 2nd ed. Bookcrafters, 1995.

Jones, V. C. *The Bull Run Campaign: First Manassas.* Conshohocken, Pa.: Eastern Acorn Press, 1981.

Manassas Garden Club Scrapbooks. Manassas, Va.: 1933–2008.

Manassas Journal Messenger selected news articles.

Manassas Museum System Files and Photograph Collections.

McCarron, Kay, and Sharon Doyle. *The Search for Tudor Hall: A Phase I and II Archeological Survey.* Manassas Va.: Manassas Museum, 1989.

McDonald, JoAnna, ed. *The Faces of Manassas.* Redondo Beach, Calif.: Rank and File Publications, 1998.

Mills, Charles A. *Echoes of Manassas.* Manassas, Va.: Friends of the Manassas Museum, 1988.

Mulvaney, Kathleen. *Manassas, A Place of Passages.* Charleston, S.C.: Arcadia Publishers, 1992.

Naisawald, VanLoan. *Manassas Junction and the Doctor.* Manassas, Va.: Lake Lithograph Inc., 1981.

Osbourn High School Yearbooks.

Parker, Kathleen A., and Jacqueline L. Hernigle. *Portici: Portrait of a Middling Plantation in Piedmont Virginia.* Washington, D.C.: National Park Service, 1990.

Perdue, Charles L., Thomas E. Barden, and Robert K. Phillips. *Weevils in the Wheat: Interviews with Virginia Ex-Slaves.* Charlottesville: University Press of Virginia, 1992.

Phinney, Lucy Walsh. *Yesterday's Schools.* Self-published, 1993.

Plaster, Roberta Hooe. Hooe Family Genealogy. Manassas Museum, 2004.

Potomac News/Manassas Journal Messenger.

Prince William County. Quebecor Books, 2002.

Prince William County Public Library System, Bull Run Regional Library Ruth E. Lloyd Information Center (RELIC) files, photographs, and the *Prince William Reliquary* quarterly online journal *Quarterly.*

Rabatin, June. *Count the Ties to Manassas.* Manassas, Va.: Manassas Museum, 1984.

Ratcliffe, R. Jackson. *This Was Manassas.* Manassas, Va.: Good Printers, 2000.

Simmons, Catherine T. *Manassas, Virginia, 1873–1973.* Manassas, Va.: REF Typesetting and Publishing Inc., 1983.

Thomas, Ann Walser Harrover. "Memories of Manassas." 2006.

Virginia Writers' Program. *The Negro in Virginia.* New York: Hastings House Publishers, 1940.

Wood, Linda S., and Richard Rabinowitz. *Coming to Manassas: Peace, War, and the Making of a Virginia Community.* New York: American Public History Laboratory, 2003.

Word from the Junction. Manassas Museum Newsletters. July 1985–2005. Manassas, Va.

Writers Program of the Virginia Work Projects Administration. *Prince William: The Story of Its People and Its Places.* Manassas, Va.: Bethlehem Club, 1988.

Index

About the Author

Rita Gibson Koman is a native of the St. Louis, Missouri, suburbs. She holds a BA in History from Coe College in Cedar Rapids, Iowa, and an MA in History earned on a William Randolph Hearst fellowship from the University of Maryland. She taught history and government at the high school and community college levels for twenty years, thirteen of which were at Osbourn High School in Manassas. She has been a history curriculum specialist since 1992 and was named an outstanding teacher by the Virginia Council for the Social Studies and the Virginia Daughters of the American Revolution.

Koman received fellowships from the National Endowment for the Humanities at the University of Kansas, the Virginia Foundation for Humanities, twice, at the University of Virginia, the Woodrow Wilson Foundation at Princeton University, and the Coe Foundation at Stanford University. Additionally, she was a fellow at the University of Virginia's Center for Public Policy as the resident teacher in state and local government for one year.

For five years, Koman has lectured on Virginia and Virginia women's history for the Osher Lifelong Learning Institute affiliated with George Mason University. For seven years, she authored "Virginia Women in History" biographies published annually for the Virginia Women in History poster by the Virginia Foundation for Women. She has had numerous articles on history with curriculum instruction published by the National Register of Historic Places, the Organization of American History's *Magazine of History*, UCLA's History Center, and in various state publications. Koman served on Virginia's State Executive Board of Delta Kappa Gamma Society International, a professional honor society of women educators, and currently serves on the Advisory Board for the *Magazine of History*. She was an early member of the Manassas Museum Associates begun in 1976 and continues to be an active museum supporter with her time. Since 1963, Koman has lived with her husband, Joseph, in Manassas where they raised their four children and have four grandchildren.